PREVIOUS PRAISE FOR BLOOD, SWEAT, TEARS & IDEAS

(as 1st Edition, The Universe Doesn't Give A Sh*t About Your Book: A Brutally Honest Guide to Self-Publishing)

"There's no BS in this book, just straightforward advice from an experienced indie author. Rachael does give a sh*t, and it's told in a pleasant and engaging manner."

Petra van der Ploeg, author of the Somnia Series

"An entertaining and informative addition to the self-publishing marketplace that demonstrates there is always space for another good book in the category. I particularly enjoyed the advice on marketing and promotion, which was well-organised and filled with important and practical tips for both real-world and online promotion."

Edwin H Rydberg, Quantum Dot Press

"Get it right first time with this time-saving, direct guide for the aspiring self-published author."

Malcolm Clarke, Durham Ct. Cll

Copyright © 2025 by Rachael Hardcastle

All rights reserved.

ISBN: 978-1-7394376-5-7

No part of this publication may be reproduced, distributed, or transmitted in any form or by any means, including photocopying, recording, or other electronic or mechanical methods, without the prior written permission of the publisher, except in the case of brief quotations embodied in critical reviews and certain other non-commercial uses permitted by copyright law.

Images and fonts used as per CCO license.

Cover and Formatting by Curious Cat Books
Copy-Editing by Curious Cat Books

For permission requests, please contact the author via their website: www.rachaelhardcastle.com

A copy of this book is available from the British Library.

Also available as an e-book.

Revised 1st Edition
Previously Published as 978-1999968878 (2021)
The Universe Doesn't Give A Sh*t About Your Book (1st Edition)

BLOOD, SWEAT, TEARS, & *Ideas*

Also Available by Rachael Hardcastle:

<u>THE CHRONICLES OF PANDORA:</u>
To See A World (1)
Of Heavens & Wild Flowers (2)
To Hold An Infinity (3)

And available (as E. Rachael Hardcastle):

Noah Finn & the Art of Suicide (1)
Noah Finn & the Art of Conception (2)

Aeon Infinitum: Run For Your Life
Bluetooth & the World Wide Web
Elemental Ascension

CONTENTS

JUST IGNORE THEM..................11
- A Little Disclaimer....................16
- How To Use This Book..............17
- Blood, Sweat, Tears & Ideas......21
- Put That in the 'Win' Column......26

IDEA GENERATION....................29
- ABC...29
- A Is For Archiving.....................30
- Writing Things Down.................30
- Remind Yourself........................32
- Scenes, Not Chapters.................32
- Journals.....................................33
- B Is For Blending......................34
- Inject Some Fun........................34
- Mix It Up...................................35
- Annotations...............................36
- What's Your Why?....................37
- Playlists.....................................38
- C Is For Cheating......................39
- Methods....................................39
- Story Beats...............................40
- The Series.................................42
- The Book..................................43
- The Chapters............................43
- Answering Plots and Subplots...45
- Other Considerations................47
- The Next Book.........................48

PUBLISHING BASICS..................51

- Step One - What Are You Doing?...............51
  - What Is Self-Publishing?.........................51
  - The Four Types..52
  - Print On Demand vs Offset Printing......54
  - Audio 56
  - Platform Comparisons............................56
  - Private Publishing...................................58
  - In Summary...58
- Step Two - Platform Considerations..........61
  - Draft2Digital..61
  - Free Books..62
  - Free Promotions - Benefits.....................64
  - Free Promotions - Limitations...............65
  - Stocking Your book.................................65
  - Second Hand Books................................68
  - Book Reviews...69
  - 50 Reviews = Success?............................72
  - Leaving Reviews......................................73
  - Review Rules..74
  - Discounting Your Book..........................78
  - Accepting Returns...................................79
  - Pre-Orders...79
- Step Three - Things You Should Know......81
  - Distributors & Wholesalers....................81
  - Copyright..82
  - First Editions..83
  - International Standard Book Number....83
  - Nielsen Title Editor.................................86
  - Legal Deposits...86
  - Category Codes.......................................88
- Step Four - Take Care of Yourself..............89

- Public Liability Insurance.......................89
- Professional Indemnity..........................89
- Journaling...90
- Success Journal.....................................92
- Positive Affirmations.............................94

PREPARATION...97

Step One - Editing.......................................97
- Hire An Editor..97
- Book and Chapter Length....................101
- Rachael's Six Read Rule......................103
- Technical Sh*t......................................106
- Types of Speech...................................107
- Punctuation Problems?........................108
- Tense & Point of View (POV).............110
- Active Vs Passive Voice......................111
- Front and Back Matter.........................112

Step Two - Formatting................................113
- Formatting is Easy?.............................113
- Creating Page Styles............................114
- Applying Page Styles..........................117
- Headers and Footers............................118
- Images..118
- Contents Page......................................120
- Bleed..120
- Additional Technical Terms.................122
- Dialogue...123
- Convenience..125

Step Three - Cover Design.........................127
- Basics...127
- Character Covers.................................129
- Dust Jackets...129

- Duplex......................................130
- Bevelled Edges..........................130
- Series.......................................130
- Summary..................................131
- Step Four - Pricing......................133
  - Basics.....................................133
  - USP..134
  - QR Codes...............................135
  - Sale or Return........................136
  - Royalties................................137
  - Charitable Donations..............139
  - Expenses................................140
  - Retailer Discounts & Returns...141
- ATTENDING EVENTS...................143
  - Organise An Event..................143
  - Setting Up E-mail Signatures...150
  - What Happens At Events........151
  - Get To Know Your Customers...151
  - Appearance............................156
  - Stock......................................162
  - Author Copies........................163
  - Second-hand Copies..............163
  - Uncontrollable Stuff...............164
  - Failure....................................165
- WORKING WITH OTHERS............169
  - External Support.....................169
  - Don't Rely On Others..............170
  - Cancellations..........................171
- MARKETING................................173
- Step One - Websites....................173
  - SEO and Keywords.................173

- Subscriptions..................................175
- Pages..175
- Domains..177
- Blogs...178
- Step Two - Social Media......................181
  - Like for Like...................................181
  - Paid Advertising.............................184
  - Making Friends...............................184
  - Hashtags..186
  - Social Media Tips...........................186
  - Summary..189
- Step Three - Paperwork.......................191
  - Press Releases...............................191
  - Mission Statements........................193
  - Press Kits......................................193
  - Marketing Plans..............................195
- Step Four - In Print.............................197
  - Bookmarks.....................................197
  - Leaflets...199
  - Business Cards..............................200
  - Signed Photos................................200
  - Sticker Rolls..................................200
- Step Five - Common Sense..................201
  - Business Hours..............................201
  - Consistency...................................202
  - Top Tip..203
  - Archery...204
  - Bestsellers....................................205
  - Trends...210
  - Final Thoughts on Marketing............211
  - Merchandise Ideas.........................214

Getting Paid Securely............................215
AND THAT'S IT... FOR NOW.................217
  Phew, Glad That's Over?......................217
  One Final Note.....................................219
RESOURCES..221
AUTHOR'S NOTE....................................224

JUST IGNORE THEM

Nobody cares about your book as much as you do. That's the truth; something you create is *always* going to mean more to you than anyone else. Before you begin what I *know* will be an amazing adventure, please try to remember that **none of what you're about to experience is personal** (but sometimes it can feel a bit that way).

If your book is finished and ready to publish, you'll know exactly how difficult writing is because you've spent months (perhaps even years!) worrying and spending time perfecting that manuscript. It doesn't matter the length, the inspiration behind it, or the genre —you've created something unique and you should be proud! Congratulations, you're already halfway there.

This is when you need to hear a crucial piece of advice: **Just ignore them.** Because it's from this point onwards that other people will get involved in what you're doing. So I'm not going to tell you the hard part is over. Honestly, it's just beginning. Some of those people you'll welcome in. Others, not so much. And I absolutely *get it*; for someone to shoot down your accomplishment in the first week of its existence? **You're allowed to feel what you're feeling.**

A lack of sales and interest in something you've worked super hard to produce can really hurt. It's also easy to take a loved one's feedback or negative reviews from strangers to heart. Some will provide you with feedback in a not-so-friendly manner, regardless of how much effort you've put into the book or how nice you've been to them. Know that 1* reviews are inevitable. Don't even try to avoid them because everyone is entitled to their opinion and you can't please some no matter what you do. Even if 90% think it's the best thing they've ever read, 10% might think it's awful. And you know what? They might be right.

This is when I'll remind you of that incredible advice. **JUST IGNORE THEM.**

If you're still writing your book (or are yet to start) and you're reading this to prepare for what's to come, this next bit is for you.

Self-publishing is (generally) not a big money-making business and it can be a very lonely job. That's not to say you won't become a huge success or make money from your writing; there are plenty of great examples out there who make a living from it. However, writing is a solitary hobby for most, even if they have a co-author. There will come a time when what's in your mind needs to meet the paper, and only *you* will know how to do that because only *you* can access your thoughts. If you're working with another, be sure to be respectful of and patient with each other —you're entering this industry together. Why not lean on and support one another?

There are lots of things every writer needs to prepare themselves to hear. Some are daft, some are offensive, and some... well, some you don't even have to entertain. I've said it before. I'll say it again.

Just Ignore Them

JUST.
IGNORE.
THEM.

Here are a few examples (and no doubt the response/s you've often dreamt of giving) to a few I've personally experienced over the years. Number 1 and 3 have to be my favourites.

1. "So you're not '*published published'* then?"

What even *is* 'published published'? Do you mean my book isn't *real* because a big publishing house didn't offer me a contract, or I'm not a *real* writer because it's not my full-time job? Do you just assume I got hundreds of rejections and I'm using self-publishing as a back-up? Here's the thing, lots of authors choose to self-publish for many reasons. Others prefer to query an agent. Some like to do a bit of both. There are many versions of this silly question. Whichever form they ask this of you, ***just ignore them.***

Or, and I *love* this one because it's the expected follow-up to the above nonsense:

2. "Don't you have a 'proper job'?"

This 'writing business' is hard work, and lots of writers have a full-time job alongside building worlds, creating characters, attending book signings and fairs, and spending hours every day marketing the finished product. If you think about it, these people are actually working *two* jobs now, thank you very much.

Just smile and nod. Oh, and *ignore them*.

Sometimes they go straight for a cringe-worthy question they don't *think* you'll have the guts to say no to. But we will. We can't blame them for trying though... right?

3. "Can I read your book? It's free, right? You can just send me a copy."

Of course they can read it, but no, it's not free. It's taken you a number of months to write, edit, design, market, and publish. It's cost you money, and is a *business*. Supermarkets don't give their produce away for free. Retailers don't give their designer clothing away for free. Why should authors give their carefully crafted hardback novels away for free? But they do occasionally if they feel pressured by friends or family. Their reasons are their own. A kind 'friends and family discount' might be a reasonable counter-offer instead?

There's always one who just doesn't 'get' creativity because they're not so easily inspired or motivated, and that's fine, until they attempt to bring you down too. **Never let anyone convince you that your passion for writing and the time you dedicate to it is pointless.** *Ignore them!*

4. "Why are you stressing over a hobby?"

You don't even have to answer that. You have my permission to grin and silently leave the room. In other words, just *bloody ignore them*.

Just Ignore Them

But there are others. Others who think you have it easy! Others who think your job is something *they* could do in a free afternoon, with one hand and their eyes closed. They could have written twenty books in the time is has taken you to finish one. Is this familiar?

4a. "How hard can it be? *I* was thinking about writing a book, but I don't have time."

You could tell them that you're dragging this process out to fill the void in your soul. You're a writer, so it's mostly dark in there anyway. That will shut them up, because they'll think you're a cave-dwelling vampire. If you want them to go away, hissing at them will probably seal the deal. Anyway, ***go ahead and ignore them.***

And finally, there are those who mean well and are perhaps a bit *too* supportive!

5. "Are you done yet?"

Well, I'd have been finished weeks ago if I didn't have to answer all these silly questions. I'll be finished when I'm finished. Sod off. Or, a rather basic 'no' will suffice.

Like me, I'm *sure* you have never responded to any of those in such a manner and nor should you (out loud). We're professional. What goes on inside your head is your business, and if you want to curse them later in the comfort of your own home, by all means have at it. But in the meantime, offer a well-rehearsed, friendly response, and **keep working hard to achieve your dreams.** Each to their own.

Remember to smile.

And to *just ignore them*.

A Little Disclaimer

I want you to take what I say on board but with a pinch of salt. I am *one* writer. I am *one* reader. I am *one* publisher. I don't make millions and I don't sell millions. And, as you know, there are many, many more out there. Therefore, I can only give you *my* opinion and advise you based on *my* experiences and the knowledge I've gained through research and practices. What I tell you in this book is also based on how I have interpreted the advice of others. The more mentors you can find, the better.

It's up to you how much of this you apply to your own journey. I actually *hate* that phrase because everything seems to be described as a 'journey' these days, but it fits what I'm trying to say here. I prefer to see this as an adventure and an opportunity to 'level up' your skill set. I'll let you decide how right or wrong you think I am. Still, until you read about my life as an author, I'm one less mentor you can learn from—the more people you speak to, the better you can decide for yourself what works and what doesn't.

I'm not a lawyer and I've never worked in a large publishing house. With regards to contracts and agreements and outsourcing jobs like editing and cover design etc., you can seek professional guidance. I have, however, had some training with regards copy-editing and self-publishing. But you can gain as many qualifications as you want; if you're not writing, then you're not a writer, and you're not going to learn. I'd also highly recommend reading. I aim for one book per month, and the subject doesn't matter (but a genre similar to what you're writing may offer better insights).

I've always been an avid reader and for several years designed covers and formatted manuscripts for authors all over the world. I've been an indie author since 2010, but writing in general for much longer. You can read more about my story in the next section.

How To Use This Book (& Stuff I Assume):

I do a lot of assuming, and I'm not going to tell you how to use this book because I hate it when other books try to tell me how to use books. You turn the pages and read, right? I'm sure you purchased this book for a reason, so I'm confident you know what you're doing here. But there are a few things I would like to say about what you're about to read. Mostly, it's *why* I wrote this book the way I did.

- I've covered what I deem to be **the basics**, and what you'll need to get started.
- I'm **assuming your book is finished and ready to go**, but I'm also assuming **you're a new writer**, meaning the manuscript you're working on now will soon become your debut release. I'm guessing it will need a lot of work and polishing as first books always do (and second, third, fourth books do, too!), so I've included

some self-editing basics for you.
- **I'm not going to teach you how to write** because that's down to repetition. **I'll explain some terms** and their meanings, though, just in case you're not already familiar.
- Think of this as a crash course and a **handy reference** for your desk, in case you forget something you think you 'probably should know by now'. Nonsense. **This sh*t is hard.**
- I've also **assumed you not only want to learn what to do, but keep your costs as low as possible**. When I first started I made a LOT of mistakes. I didn't invest in things I should have and I didn't learn as much as I needed to prior to releasing my debut. I probably spent money in the wrong places and on the wrong things. I didn't research as thoroughly as I should have. I hold up my hands and admit it, which is why '*The Soul Sanctuary*' (2010) is no longer in print. So, I've decided to *assume* (there I go again) that you're in the same position I was. I'll show you some free and easy ways to format your book and design a cover professionally, allowing you to avoid the mistakes I made.

Check out the contents page for an overview of what's included and you'll see how I've structured each section. We'll start with the basics, then preparation, then move on to marketing which I'm not going to lie makes *my* head hurt. I hope it's easy to follow and understand, though.

At the back, I've collated a list of useful links for

you to use as a quick reference point, too. I'm not into these huge bibliographies and indexes you see in non-fiction books, though, plus I want you to read the whole thing, so the contents page is your map. And I've written this in a very 'brain dump' kind of way, whereby I've emptied my mind of anything I could think a first-time indie author might need to know, then explained as well as I can.

You might find it overwhelming and, after a few chapters, decide you can't be bothered with all this fuss. Self-publishing isn't for you, then. Please try to stick with it for a few more chapters, because whilst I'll make this sound like hard work in hell, **it's *so* rewarding and fulfilling knowing your success is down to *you*.**

I decided to write the first edition of this book for one very important reason: when I started publishing, I wish *I* had a book like this to guide me, honestly, through what it's like to be an indie author. **It's bloody hard work, but it's also immense fun.** I'm re-releasing it now because processes and technologies move on, and I wanted my advice to be current.

I was so overwhelmed back in 2010 with the various platforms, terminology, rules, laws and opportunities that, to be honest, it was frustrating and sometimes upsetting. I wanted so badly to be a popular writer that I skimped on quality and did things wrong because I didn't know any better; making mistakes, however, is why I'm where I am today. **Mistakes made me work harder** to fix them, to please my readers and myself. I don't regret any of them. I'd make those mistakes again in a heartbeat. That's why I'm sharing them with you, so you'll be one step ahead of the author I was at 18. Sure, you'll make mistakes of your own and that's fine, too. Then, when you're offering advice to others, you can pay your experiences and successes forward.

The brutal part of this book is learning about failure and setbacks because we can't all be mega-successful all of the time. **Success is in the smallest of goals we meet, in the readers we shake hands with and in the books we sign.** Whilst I've tried to write as positively as I can, some chapters may still grind your bones. But, that's just part of self-publishing—**we pick ourselves up, dust ourselves off, and crack on.**

Another uncomfortable part of this book is in the volume of stuff you should know. I've said it before, I'll say it again: if you don't want to know, you shouldn't be self-publishing. Doing things your own way is different to ignoring the basic requirements—the last thing I want is to preach that things must be done a certain way because you will absolutely discover your own methods and hacks. And *that's* OK. Just don't jump in head-first at the shallow end of the pool without your bathing suit on.

Finally, you're probably wondering why this book was originally called '*The* Universe *Doesn't Give A Sh*t About Your Book*'. I'm an anxious person. Writing helps with my troubles but my troubles fuel my writing; they've led me to read lots of self-help and personal development books, most of which encourage sending out positive thoughts, energy, and vibes into the universe to receive success and the life I want and feel I deserve in return.

Years later, I still have anxiety.

To some extent, I *do* believe positive thinking helps us succeed. That's why I practice mindfulness, meditation and journaling. Whilst I expect they will aid my anxiety and leave me feeling inspired and calmer, I *don't* expect them to make my book a bestseller. There is a tiny bit in the self-care section of this book about positive affirmations and journaling, but generally, I think all this 'send out positivity to receive everything you've ever wanted' stuff is mostly BS. Sorry.

The universe won't reward authors who hit 'publish' and do naff all to sell their book—wishing and hoping it sells isn't enough. **The universe rewards hard work** (though I would argue you reward yourself —after all, *you've* done the work), so I originally named my book after the way I *used* to think success would breed. Now, though, I think it's important to recognise that **writing and publishing your own book involves a lot of blood, sweat, tears and, obviously, good ideas.**

And that's it, really.

Write on, you've got this.

Blood, Sweat, Tears & Ideas

My name is Rachael Hardcastle. I'm an Amazon #1 bestselling author of several titles in two countries. I've been writing and self-publishing since I was a teen, and released my debut in 2010. I'm very pleased to meet you.

I started my publishing company *Curious Cat Books* (CCB) in 2017 so I could help others but mostly,

I write as a hobby; it's something I have always enjoyed and it allows me to be creative, and to share that creativity with other people. In doing so, **I can entertain them, I can teach them, and I can give them messages based on my morals, values, and experiences.**

In 2009, I completed the first draft of my debut novel, *The Soul Sanctuary*. I was 18. I queried publishing the book with agents and publishing houses (as you seem expected to do when you're new to this industry) and got nowhere. Feedback was positive, but I struggled to find anyone I could trust with my manuscript. So my dad suggested I look into 'self-publishing'. He said if I could get the book to a high standard on the inside, we could use print-on-demand (POD) platforms on the internet to publish the book without a big publishing house's help.

A POD company would print one book for one customer's order, so there would be no upfront fees or storage costs for books printed in advance (also a bit better for the environment?). Higher royalties, creative control, and the ability to design the book myself. This was exciting!

Dad used his computer skills to design my front cover using royalty-free images, and I used editing software to copy-edit and proofread the book. We then created a free account with a POD website, uploaded the files, and hit 'publish'. I ordered a single copy to check I was 100% happy with it before it became available to the public, and I got a delivery confirmation email during a free period at school. I drove home to collect it with a friend in the passenger seat.

I opened it in the car. **I cried.**

I was *so proud* and so impressed with the finished product. My friend was horrified, thinking I hated what I was seeing when actually, I was in love. Students and teachers bought copies. I was suddenly 'that published author'. I felt like a rock star.

A year or two later, I decided to give traditional publishing another go, wondering if the grass would be greener. I have always admired traditionally published authors and been in awe of the process and their successes. I queried a few agents for a new book I had written, and finally, somebody agreed to take me on. He said he was 'doing me a favour', but after 12 months, we hadn't progressed. When I challenged a lack of communication, he asked me for money to copy-edit the novel himself as it was 'not to standard', despite the complimentary feedback he said the publishers were providing. I walked away feeling a little deflated, scammed of my time and energy (but thankfully not out of any money).

After writing and publishing a few more books, I discovered other platforms, new techniques, systems, and software to improve them. I trained as a copy-editor myself so I could thoroughly and professionally perfect my manuscripts. I re-created and re-published some, and took my debut title 'out of print' realising there were many things I'd done wrong. I was sad not to have a big publisher behind me, but loving the ability to change and improve as my knowledge grew. There was always the option to be a hybrid author in the future.

Nothing is impossible.

In 2016, I started to expand by visiting schools and organisations. My old primary school invited me in to work with their Year 6 students, and together we wrote and published two short story books. Thinking absolutely nothing would come of it, I e-mailed *Made In Leeds* and heard back almost straight away—they wanted to feature us on a TV programme! I never thought I would be on television because of my books.

The year after, having had a taste of what it felt like to help create other authors, I met a writer with Dyslexia who attended a creative writing course I was running in a community centre. She was trying to find ways to connect with others and get out of her comfort zone, and she had written a children's book. After hearing her story and her motivations, I signed her as the first CCB author, and together we created her debut.

When her book was released later that year, she cried. I got her reaction on video. **It was beautiful.**

More. I wanted to do more of this. But, the best was yet to come. And 2017 would be an amazing year.

The local Lord Mayor attended a book signing I was running during a Christmas market. I'd emailed him thinking it was a long shot, but he said yes, then left with one of my books. I asked him a few business questions during the event and he kindly invited me to share some tips over tea at Town Hall. **I said YES**. And it wasn't long after that I had my first live interview with a radio station which turned out to be in Detroit, USA. The host invited me back several times following that interview, and this led to lots of other stations interviewing me, including BBC Leeds, between 2017 and 2020.

By this time, I had several authors signed to CCB, all with books either published already or due for release, I'd co-written a children's book with my father (more on this later), and I'd been on my first ever WHSmiths book tour in Yorkshire.

I saw my books on physical book shelves in real stores. **I cried... again!** I do that a lot, obviously.

Then one day, I was out shopping with my mother in Waterstones, Bradford. Too nervous to do it myself, she approached the desk and asked for the manager. I was so embarrassed, but he was a lovely guy, and because I was a local, he offered to book me in his diary for a chat about how we could work together. I left the store on cloud 9, but I never expected he would actually help me. The meeting came and he opened the conversation by asking me, nicely, what I wanted from our meeting. I stammered, shoved aside the masses of figures and paperwork I had collated on CCB's book sales so far, then said as confidently as I could muster that I wanted a working relationship, some books in the store, and an event or signing held there for my company.

His response? A smile, a nod, and a cheerful "done." I left the store with a HUGE smile on my face, and, that's right, **I CRIED again** in my car.

I am grateful for his kindness every day.

In October 2021, I planned, organised, and hosted that event in Waterstones, Bradford—a store I had only ever dreamed of seeing my books in. When I told people I wanted it to be a fairly formal event, some rolled their eyes and said, 'nah, that's not going to work'. So **I made it work** and hosted the event I had envisioned. I invited the media, Lord Mayors from local areas, other authors, local businesses and more, and we had a huge turnout despite having to re-schedule once following the Covid-19 pandemic.

I didn't know at the time, but I was actually pregnant with my son during the event. I knew my focus needed to be on my family, so I decided to take a step back from publishing for others when he was born. I hoped I had taught them everything they needed to know to make it and to inspire them to keep going.

And here we are today. I'm **still writing**, **still dreaming** of being a hybrid author at some point in the future, and **still on a mission to inspire others** to follow in my footsteps.

Put That in the 'Win' Column...

I have and will always believe that 'success' is in the little wins; wins that stay with you and are meaningful because they were unplanned.

On my lunch breaks, I would sometimes walk up to my parents' house for coffee with my dad, David. He told me about a strange dream he'd had, where an idea for a children's book came to him: spiders running the World Wide Web. My dad had written the story in note-form, created the funny characters he'd based off our beloved relatives, and used his humour to give them names. His creativity was running wild, so we decided that with his imagination and my writing and publishing experience, we could co-write a children's book which we later titled, *Bluetooth & the World Wide Web*.

But my dad's ideas were adult and sometimes a bit... inappropriate? There was lots of 'Dad, we can't say that' and 'Dad, we might get sued.' We laughed a lot, and we argued a little over some of my edits because there was plenty of red pen. When it came to hiring an illustrator, we disagreed again because we loved every sample and couldn't decide.

Eventually, we settled on a Halifax-based artist and she designed one of my favourite characters.

His name was Pond. Fleadrick Pond.

We wanted our book to be a family-friendly, fun bedtime story parents and children could enjoy together. But we also wanted to give a respectful nod of the head to our influences growing up (such as Morcambe and Wise), and to family who had passed. We re-created my grandfather as a centipede, we turned my dad's cousin into a beetle-spraying mechanic, and we decided to bring my great uncle to life in the form of a miserable, snail-riding flea named 'Fleadrick Pond'. My uncle Fred fell in love with the idea, honoured, I think, in his own way. When we gifted him a copy, he couldn't wait to show everybody in the nursing home how he would live forever as Fleadrick. He was so proud.

We then had a toy made and when Fred passed away; we kept it as a wonderful memory of what a grumpy (but loveable) guy he truly was! Somewhere out there, I imagine there are other father-daughter duos just waiting to be inspired, and I hope to be the one to give them that much-needed nudge.

When what you do means something to someone, it's automatically a win. And if anyone tries to tell you otherwise... *just ignore them!*

Writing and publishing a book yourself is an immensely fulfilling and empowering accomplishment. Exploring this industry will not only expand your knowledge of a new skill/hobby, but **it will open your mind and your heart to an incredible way to express yourself**, and keeping a journal to document your journey is like free self-therapy.

I am always so proud of the work I put in, no matter how well the book sells or what the reviews say, and there is no way to please everyone (nor would I want or expect to). Because **writing must first bring *me* joy.** I hope the product of that, in turn, brings you joy too.

Thank you for allowing me to share my passion with you.

IDEA GENERATION

ABC

You've decided to write a book, but you're not sure where to start or if your ideas are good enough. Well, I truly believe that **the best ideas are born from our humanity—emotions, experiences, insights and everyday interactions.** Writers are sponges; it's our job to soak in everything we see and experience, and re-form or re-shape them so they work to our advantage.

Our lives are only interesting to others when we're at either end of the scale—when we hit rock bottom, or we become incredibly successful. We're up or we're down. That's why you find the best and most addictive books tend to focus on what makes humans dreadful, or what makes us incredible. There's always drama and excitement. We're suffering or at war or surviving a plague or getting over a broken heart. We're winning the lottery or falling in love or discovering we have magical powers or saving the world. What happens in between isn't interesting. Our everyday lives are not unique. Daily routines do not act as first-chapter hooks, cliffhangers, or plot twists.

Realising this, I developed a three-step process for

generating and developing new and interesting ideas based on simply being a human being. You can live your life and use these techniques. It's called the 'ABC method'. Let's get stuck in.

A Is For Archiving

Archiving is a way to keep track of yourself and the things going on around you, so you don't forget anything that may be of value later down the line.

Think about all the times you've been inspired when you're in the bathtub or driving your children to school. You missed the opportunity to make a note and it drifted from your mind because you got distracted with everyday things. Perhaps you've had a few wacky dreams (that with a bit of time and patience, may have made wonderful story ideas), but you forget everything when you woke up. Are you creating stunning scenery in your head *before* you fall asleep, and promise yourself you'll remember in the morning?

But you won't. You know you won't. You never do. And so you sacrifice them for an extra few minutes in bed. Now they're gone forever.

Writing Things Down

This is why step one (A – Archiving) is basic. It takes us to the root of the problem. To generate ideas, we must first learn to better capture and document our lives and the things that help to build those great ideas. And we can do this in a variety of

Generating Ideas

ways.

Firstly, write things down. Keep a notebook by the bed and a voice app handy on your phone. This sounds like obvious advice, but you'd be surprised how many writers can never find a pen (especially one that's working!) when they need it in an emergency. I often carry several just in case.

Some authors dislike writing their ideas down, because they're afraid they will then focus on the wrong one/s and waste time. No time writing is wasted or pointless, because it's all experience and practice. That's why, generally, I find writing down those initial early-stage ideas is beneficial, and if something pesters me or I'm still thinking about it days later, *then* I assume it's worth developing. If not, I haven't lost anything.

Hoarding memorabilia and taking photographs is the next step. This might include postcards with pictures of places that inspired you; somewhere that would make a pretty setting for a story. Learn to regularly flick through and review these items whether it's physically or in a file on your device. Consider purchasing a low-cost handheld thermal printer so you can easily stick any photos you take into a journal. Or you may want to cut out newspaper or magazine articles that have helped you, and pictures of celebrities and/or models from catalogues as character inspiration.

You will only notice you need something after you've thrown it away. So, designate one file or box for your 'hoarded' items and keep that space as tidy as you can. (I use the term 'hoarded' rather than 'collected', but collecting bits and pieces that encourage you is what I mean). Then when you struggle to come up with an idea or need something fast, reach for one of these items and think about what motivated you to keep it. For example, the location, the people, the emotions.

If you're absolutely sure it's of no use and you cannot remember why you chose to save it in the first place, it's then time to discard it.

Remind Yourself

You may simply struggle to continue to be productive after a successful few hours of writing. If you're getting weary and coming to the end of the day, but you know what's going to happen in the next chapter (or have an idea), write a short note to yourself in the document, like a 'to-do' list. This prevents you from wasting time re-reading the previous day's work. If you did, you would spend less time writing your new scenes. Know exactly what your tasks are for that day so you can complete them and repeat the process.

Scenes, Not Chapters

Are you often overwhelmed with the thought of having to write an entire chapter when you're staring at a blank screen? You're not the only one. My advice is to **write scene by scene, not chapter by chapter**. It's *much* harder to motivate yourself when you're faced with several pages.

But if you know you only have to get your character from one building to another, your target is suddenly much nearer and more achievable. You may find that by working this way, you're less distracted. Focus on one scene for now, then the next, until your chapter is completed. This will help your ideas and imagination to flow more freely, creating wholesome and believable scenes that hold a reader's attention.

Don't worry about something that hasn't happened yet! Get your character to that bridge before you try to figure out how they will cross it.

Journals

Learn to document your day, at the end of each day, so you can form a log of everything I've covered in this section so far. I previously kept a 'success journal' for anything writing and publishing related where I wrote about ideas, stuck in photos, logged sales and dimensions; anything at all related to your life as a writer can go in one place. Use an index at the front and page numbers on the bottom or flags/tabs to keep track of where everything can be found.

For this type of journaling, I use a 'bullet journal' style with dotted or squared pages and I've previously used both the Moleskine and Leuchtturm 1917 brands, but lines are fine too. Use a notebook you are attracted to, that's easy to use and comfortable, that makes you *want* to pick it up every day, and form the habit of writing a short entry on an evening before bed to get everything out of your mind. You may wish to write down anything you remember from dreams and nightmares before you start the day, too.

There are lots of ways journaling can help you to generate and develop ideas, and this overlaps into the second section.

B Is For Blending

Here I am referring to a blend of inspiration and hard work (and persistence!). Writers write, and it takes more than a short burst of energy one weekend with a cup of coffee to finish a novel. It takes time and energy over a long period of time, and it means showing up sometimes when you don't really want to. You can treat writing like a hobby or a job; I try to find a comfortable middle ground. Writing is something I enjoy, and I do not want to ruin it by forcing myself to hate the act. But, I also want to get the words on the page.

Inject Some Fun

There are many ways to force a productive mindset, starting with a fun challenge or a sprint.

You do *not* need to focus on quality, only quantity, in the early drafts. Ideas can be bland and boring and you can backfill with research later. Just get the initial bare bones down.

Alternatively, story cubes and prompts are a fun way to take the pressure off, and blend a bit of fun with the project you are working on. I have Rory's Story Cubes and use them at workshops often. These are white dice with themed images on. Then, you can use those pictures or something they inspire within you in the story you are working on. For example, if you're writing a crime and you can't decide on the murder weapon, throw the cubes. You may get a shoe, a flower, and a vampire bat. Can you come up with a weapon using one or all of those?

Of course that may sound ridiculous, and you don't have to use whatever you come up with, but the activity will teach you how to find and use the *ah-ha!* moments, and force you to take the process a little less seriously. Some story cubes are for children and intended as a game to help them improve their creative writing skills, but there is no reason why they cannot help adults too.

Story cubes come in themed packs, so depending on your genre, you can change the set you're using.

Mix It Up

Blending is also about learning to swirl your ideas with another's. And of course, I do not mean you should be stealing the plot of a bestseller. Instead, write down all the things you love about the genre you're writing, and ways that other writers have approached the subject. Choose your favourite aspects, and create something new and exciting, putting your own spin on things, having educated yourself with what's already out there.

Elizabeth Gilbert's book *Big Magic* is one of my favourites. Gilbert says that ideas come to us, and if we do nothing with them, they may move on. It helped me to see ideas as living things working to a deadline; I have to appreciate that their schedule may not work with mine, so it's OK for us to part ways sometimes.

I think this is why occasionally we come across new books that have a similar vibe to what we're currently working on; we feel as if the story was stolen or is just too similar to continue. We get disappointed and disheartened. We kick ourselves because we didn't finish the manuscript sooner.

Tell yourself that **their story is not *your* story**—remember, there are lots of zombie books and movies and TV shows, and each one creates a new breed, a new virus, and a new cause to keep fans of the genre interested.

Annotations

In my journal, I often 'annotate' movies and TV shows, and I discovered a use for this type of note-taking when re-watching The Walking Dead. I had already seen the series before, and I enjoy cheesy zombie movies too, but one day when re-watching season one of the show, I noticed a few interesting things I decided to write down in case I wanted to write my own apocalyptic book in the future (preparing me for *blending*).

I wondered why, in the early seasons, the dead are able to use tools and hold/carry items, when in the later seasons, they cannot. After chatting with another fan of the show, they told me there was a change of director, who decided to switch things up a bit. It had nothing to do with continuation or evolution, but it certainly helped me to decide what type of zombie I'd want to write and why, and how keeping things consistent was important to me.

So be a sponge and soak in as many different styles and versions as you can. Make copious notes about what types of zombies there are, the causes, symptoms, their speed, what they eat, etc. Is the story about survival or the wider plots and politics around the apocalyptic event itself?

When annotating TV shows, you can write the title, series and episode in the margin. For example, 'TWD S2 E1' stands for *The Walking Dead, Season 2, Episode 1*. Then, you would write what comes to mind, what you've noticed, what you like and dislike and more before moving on to the next.

What's Your Why?

Why are you writing what you're writing? If you're struggling to generate ideas for your sci-fi novel, is it because you love science fiction but you know nothing about science or world building, or is it because you know a lot about those things and are a bit bored? Is the research too overwhelming, or do you wish there was more to learn? Backtrack and re-think. You may be spending too much time trying to study the genre. Sometimes, it is easier to write the story and use a placeholder mid-chapter or even mid-paragraph such as *'[insert science research here]'* and then carry on until you have a completed manuscript. Then, you can flesh out later.

The same sometimes goes for those who have been told to write what they know. They spend so much time writing a boring crime fiction because they used to be a police man. They don't watch crime shows or read murder mysteries because they have spent time doing the job, and so they read fantasy instead for a refreshing change. So, why would they write crime? Because somebody told them they should. Because they know the genre and don't need to research. But, the writer is bored, and the ideas and passion are flat.

If this is you, backtrack. Are you writing this story because you want to, or do you *really* want to be writing erotica? It's easier and more fun to write something you love and are excited about; ideas flow freely and generate themselves when we are deeply involved in a project and thoroughly enjoying it. One sentence sparks the idea for another, characters hold conversations through us, and we suddenly find ourselves three chapters in.

Playlists

Blend music into your writing habits, too. I've put together Spotify playlists of tracks I think will spark ideas and inspiration for me when writing certain genres, and I find I am always sucked into that world when the theme music is well chosen. For me, instrumental music usually works the best.

I really enjoyed The Pirates of the Caribbean, and it has a lot to do with the music which perfectly compliments the action. Can you imagine your favourite movies without the epic soundtrack? Would they have the same impact, or strike up the same emotions?

Generating Ideas

Imagine a serious scene that requires sombre music being played over a children's song. Certain pieces of music are simply magical—they transport you and promote that imagery. If you want to feel 'in the zone' when writing your book, try creating a Spotify playlist. You could even share it to promote your book when it releases.

C Is For Cheating

There are a few ways you can 'cheat' if you are *really* struggling to generate ideas, and I will say again here that this is not the same thing as blending, and we are certainly not ripping off another author's work.

Methods

Let's start by picking up some reference books. The first is a collection of basic ideas you can explore in your own way. The second and third are filled with prompts and inspiration.

1. *The Writer's Idea Thesaurus* by Fred D White
2. *The Writers Idea Book* by Jack Heffron
3. *The Writers Idea Workshop* by Jack Heffron

Use an idea reference book like *The Writer's Idea Thesaurus* to select a story idea that interests you, then mind map what you could do with it, or things you have already seen done. From there, you can blend and brew something fresh. You are not stealing anyone's hard-work, merely choosing a popular theme at random and seeing how you can re-brand it.

I have found the use of tarot cards to be helpful in planning a character's journey and arc. I did this in Elemental Ascension as there are fortune-tellers in the world I created. I found studying the character archetypes from *The Hero's Journey* by Christopher Vogler to be a huge help in understanding the expected roles certain characters play, and also how best to apply the three-act structure. This is sometimes also known as the writer's journey or the *Monomyth* by Joseph Campbell.

If you are stuck in a specific place, unsure what needs to happen next, look at the next natural/expected step based on the three-act structure and the various archetypes and stages within them.

Finally, we can take things back to basics again with a simple spider diagram. Spider diagrams or mind maps are fantastic tools for developing your ideas and expanding on them. Simply put the title in the centre, then branch out into story, setting, characters, subplots and more, then branch off again to jot down your thoughts.

It's that easy.

Story Beats

If you struggle when writing a series to keep all your ideas, plots, sub-plots, character arcs, descriptions, timelines and more in order, you may therefore be spending too much time trying to revise and organise what you've already written instead of

Generating Ideas

working on the next one. It can be difficult to remember everything or to ensure all the questions are answered. I was guilty of this, so I devised a version of a 'story beats' tool you may already be familiar with—a term used to describe sometimes small but important parts of the story that act as the foundation, where things take an interesting or notable turn. These can be the twists and turns, emotional revelations or incidents that shift the story's direction.

After writing my '*Finding Pandora*' series in 2010 (now *The Chronicles of Pandora*), I realised I was guilty of the above. The series is rich with magic, different species and cultures, rules and sub-plots that intertwine, and lots of characters. There *had* to be a way to sort through everything to make it easy to find and navigate; this would hopefully prevent me having to re-read the previous novels to get myself up to speed and also save me time and effort (sweat and tears).

And so, my version of 'story beats' was born, and usually when I explain how and why I do things this way during a talk or a workshop, initially I'm met with puzzled and concerned faces due to the sheer volume of work and words this process involves (to begin with). Because once you're up and running, my story beats method is a life-saver, so I'm going to teach you the basics. Note here that I create and add to my story beats when the initial first draft is done (so *after* I have written the book). I'll explain why as we go through.

Begin with book one in your series. You've already written this book, so these steps should be easy if a little time-consuming. When you've completed book one, you will see how this works.

Stick with the process. It's worth it.
I promise.

The Series

Open a Word document (or any other system like Scrivener) and on the first page you are going to write the title of the series you're writing. For me, this would be '*The Chronicles of Pandora*'. You can then, beneath it, include any reference material like the ISBN, a picture of the book cover/s in order, the blurb/s from the back in order, or any quotes/poems the series includes or is inspired by. If you know what all the other books in the series are called, you can use bullet points on this page to list them (again, in order).

You will then need to choose three or four colours. We're going to create a key, and mine included orange for important information/must remember, red for plots and sub-plots, and black for everything else. You may wish to add an extra colour if there's something else you struggle to monitor, for example blue for the timeline. It's up to you. You don't need to use this key until you get to the chapters section.

In the series section, don't forget to include maps, signs and symbols and their meanings, a cheat sheet for all the supernatural powers or species in the series, and of course a list of all the characters and their descriptions. I tend to list these in order of their appearance during the series, formatted like this: *Name, Species/Power, Physical Description, Family Connections, Job/Role.*

Generating Ideas

The Book

Book one is naturally going to be the first book you break down, so the first page should be the book's cover and if it helps you, the blurb and the ISBN (anything that's relevant *only* to this title).

You can do this for every book in your series. Mine is the equivalent of a book cover on one side of the page and the details on the back—one sheet of paper is all you need here, because the next section is what's important.

The Chapters

Begin with the heading 'Chapter One' (and/or the title of the chapter if you use these). If the book is set in a specific year or you have a timeline or a countdown clock, write next to the chapter heading where you are. For example, '*Chapter One – January 2025*'.

Now re-read your first chapter and make notes as you go through. What happens? Where are we and what does the setting look like? Which characters do we meet and what do they look like? Is there anything going on in this chapter that should be remembered or is important for you as a reference? Are there any plots opened or sub-plots, like breadcrumbs dropped for later down the line?

Once you have made notes, go back and colour code them. You may also want to use short codes that you can search later (CTRL F to open a search), for example DESC for description or even, DESC followed by the character's initials if you're looking specifically for their notes. In my story I would use DESCAM for 'description of Arriette Monroe'.

Even though you have only just opened the book, if you identify a plot or a subplot, highlight that in pink and fully explain what happens later as well. This means that no matter where you pick up on this throughout your notes, it's explained in full (so there is no need to flick through to collect the stages of the plot; it's all in one place no matter where you are).

Normal summary text should be in black. Descriptions and things to remember go in orange. Plots and subplots in red. That's if you're using the same colours I do.

As an example, the first chapter of *The Chronicles of Pandora* in book one *To See A World* is a prologue, where Pandora is hiding her box within the labyrinth. Pandora's description is in orange marked up with the code DESCPB (description of Pandora's Box). I've then made a note for my own benefit in orange (of important things) about what the box contains, followed by a pink paragraph explaining how this is relevant and vital for the rest of the story.

And that's chapter one completed.

Move on to chapter two and do the same thing: '*Chapter Two – 100 Years Later (2125)*' for example. You may be tempted to want to tie any notes from this chapter in with the first, but try to refrain from noting anything backwards. If you've written your notes for chapter one in enough depth, that will suffice. By this, I mean if you make notes for a village in chapter one, don't be tempted to make those same notes again in chapter two unless it's about a new location. It's only helpful to repeat notes on a basic level when it relates to complex plots and subplots.

You may find that with the introduction of powers, species, planets etc. that your notes become thicker for the chapters where they first appear. That's fine. Your chapter notes can be as long and detailed as you wish to make them. In *The Chronicles of Pandora*, some of the characters speak Haeyloian, so I have sections throughout for translations and symbolism. Those notes are longer for that reason.

This may all seem like overkill and it absolutely is, but you are not only recapping and teaching yourself about the world you've created here; you're effectively adding a whole extra book to the series. Because, believe me, your word count for the beats alone by the end of this process will be 40k+... *easily*. This is going to be your cheat sheet. Your origin story. Your history book. Try to think of yourself as a stranger; imagine you have never encountered this series before and are examining it for the first time.

You're going to work your way to the end of book one, then something key is going to happen.

Answering Plots and Subplots

Print what you have (if you can) or open a copy of it on a second screen. You'll need this new page and what you've done already side-by-side if you can. I bind mine to create an A4 book that lives on my desk and acts as my go-to reference. I can add to it or edit it. It prevents me having to switch screens to access my notes, so I'm not distracted unless it's for research purposes.

Flick through what you've got so far and copy/paste (or summarise, whichever is best for you) the plots and sub-plots from that first book in the series on the new page. If you can do this in a chart-style, have two columns. The first for the plot itself and the second is to mark whether or not that plot/subplot is resolved during that book.

I'll give you an example. Your main character discovers they were adopted in chapter five. They don't know who their biological parents are. Do we find out before the end of book one, or is this something that's carried over into book two?

If it's a book one sub-plot, all answered and finished, then tick it or use an X on your computer. If not, leave it blank.

When you begin your notes for book two, after the cover and basic info page, you're going to migrate those unfinished plots/subplots across to the next book, which will act as a reminder that there are questions left unanswered and your readers will be angry if they are never resolved.

I have lots of plots/subplots that are resolved within the same book. Some go across one or two. Some will be answered in the final novel. But this method ensures that they *will* be answered one way or another. If you get to the end of a series and you have unticked boxes, you've got more work to do.

When you get to the end of book two, begin that summary with the plots/subplots you carried over before you add the new ones from book two. Repeat this process until you get to the final novel in your series.

Other Considerations

There are lots of additional things you can add to your story beats, and these can be in any format you want or need to make life easier for you.

Here are a few considerations:
- Character sketches or images.
  If your protagonist has lots of tattoos, why not include the outline of a human body and mark exactly where and what they are on that, a little like a map?
- Location sketches or images
  Maps are ideal here, but so are photocopies of your hand-drawn sketches or directions. I have a (basic!) battlefield plan included in mine.
- Family trees
- Timelines
- Translations (either of your own language or an existing one)
- Research
  If your novel takes place on a pirate ship, why not include research here? Do you have images of the ship you're basing it off, and are the parts all named/identified?
- Terminology
- Signs and Symbols

The Next Book

You may still be writing the series, and need these story beats in order to finish it. In these circumstances, I would advise that when you bind your notes, you do so in reverse order. I use a spiral binding for my notes created with a machine. It punches the pages, which I then hook over the spiral using a lever. It opens and closes so I can add things in and take things out, but you can use a ring folder or staples too.

You do not necessarily need to print and bind the pages in reverse order, but at least bind book one in full at the back, then book two in front of it and so on. It's up to you, though. If you'd rather have the chapters running in order, backwards it is! It's simpler then to add your new notes for each chapter you write on top to keep your story beats up-to-date. The latest action is then right at the front for you to access swiftly, ready for you to pick up where you left off.

Also, don't be afraid to scribble on your printed version or add sticky notes. I would suggest, however, that if you amend anything major that you also reflect this on your saved computer version. You can use CTRL F to locate something quickly on that document, but you cannot do that with a print-out unless you use page tabs and/or an index with page numbers. Also fine, by the way. Try to mirror them as much as you can so you're not using old notes. That character may have initially had blonde hair, but if you've changed her to a brunette and given her a piercing, you'll want to remember for continuity.

Generating Ideas

Finally, I also have one page where I use bullet points to list ideas for the next book or things I *really* want to remember. Perhaps I have questions I want to answer that don't directly relate to the plots/subplots, or I have a fantastic idea for a twist that I haven't yet written. This is an ideal place to dump all that, and of course this page will likely be covered in your handwritten notes and scribbles.

Exhausted? Me too.
It's a *long* process, but having this level of knowledge about your world-building, plot, and characters gets you ahead of the game for the next book/s in that series. It keeps the massive volume of information organised and easily accessible and gets everything out of your head, meaning you're less likely to fall victim to confusion, overwhelm and exhaustion.
Go ahead and get started. I'll wait.
Oh, and you're welcome!

PUBLISHING BASICS

Step One - What Are You Doing?

Welcome to the world of self-publishing! You've finished writing your book and are ready to polish and publish it. In this chapter, I'll be covering the answers to some common questions and concerns:

- *I just want to publish the book so friends and family can read it.*

- *I didn't know there was a difference between self-publishing and traditional publishing.*

- *I've heard so many horror stories about self-publishing. I'm scared and overwhelmed.*

What Is Self-Publishing?

To put your mind at ease and start at the very beginning, let's look at what self-publishing actually is. Self-publishing (or independent publishing) is when an author publishes their work without the involvement of an established publishing house. The unfinished manuscript you're holding now (and if you're not holding it you're probably looking at it or thinking about it lovingly) can take one of three routes.

There are three types of self-publishing platform you should be aware of before you decide to go indie—four if you include traditional publishing, though it's not indie-related. Sometimes, you can become a 'hybrid' and mix-and-match the platforms you use.

But, what are the benefits of self-publishing specifically? Well, if you'd like to keep creative control of your book, set and work to your own deadlines, outsource to professionals of your choice, and potentially earn higher royalties, then this could be the option for you. However, self-publishing doesn't come with the contacts and reach available through traditional publishing, nor does it offer an advance in royalties. It's bloody hard work, and there's a lot to learn.

The Four Types

"I didn't even know there was a difference between self-publishing and traditional publishing! I just thought published meant published!"

1. **Vanity:** When an author pays up-front for publishing services. Vanity press companies can prey on an author's ego, so costs are usually unrealistic. Many authors complain they aren't as involved in the process as they'd like to be or

Publishing Basics

are disappointed with the end product. I've heard a few horror stories, but I've also heard lots of success stories. It's personal taste, and if you're not confident to do things yourself or hire the right people, paying a company to do this on your behalf may just suit you.

2. **Digital:** When an author decides to publish an e-book (or audiobook) only using a platform such as Amazon KDP (which stands for Kindle Direct Publishing) or Draft2Digital (aka D2D). Sometimes shorter books may prove too expensive to produce as a paperback, so it's easier to release it as an e-book first. ACX is the Amazon-owned platform for audiobooks.

3. **Print on Demand (POD):** These are the self-publishing platforms that guide you through the process step-by-step and require you to upload your documents to their system, which they then print as/when an order comes in. Lots of POD platforms are free when you create an account, but some charge when you upload a document. Charges are usually small and reasonable, though, and you'll pay for any copies of the book you order.

4. **Traditional Publishing.** When the author gains an agent first, who then pitches the book to larger publishing houses which may include the 'big five'*. Some houses will accept *unsolicited* manuscripts (pitches direct from the author). If

you're interested in this route, take a look at *The Writers and Artists Yearbook* for an up to date catalogue of companies.

*For reference, the 'big five' publishing houses are currently Macmillan, Simon & Schuster, Hachette, HarperCollins and Penguin Random House. In the past, they were known as the 'big six' before Penguin and Random House merged.

You should judge the benefits of each POD platform against the price—sometimes the free platforms aren't always the best. You will be expected to purchase any copies of the book you'd like to keep for yourself and of course the files you upload should have been edited and fully formatted to meet their specifications. We'll look at editing and formatting later.

Of the types of publishing platform listed above, I'd recommend using POD—I use a combination of POD and digital.

Most POD platforms now offer e-book options so you can keep everything in one place, but if you'd like to test a book's popularity or create a free giveaway to help promote a business, then digital might be a good place to start.

Print On Demand vs Offset Printing

"I've heard so many horror stories about self-publishing, I'm scared and overwhelmed by what goes on behind the scenes."

Publishing Basics

If you're self-publishing, Print on Demand or POD will be a term you'll hear often. POD is exactly what it says on the label—printing one copy of the book to meet the demand of each customer.

For example, if you were to buy one of my fiction books from Amazon then either Amazon KDP or Ingramspark (aka the printer) would produce one copy and ship that one copy to you to meet that demand. I use more than one printer, but that's up to you. It applies to larger quantities too, for example, 100 or 1,000 books.

Though POD has gained a bad reputation in the self-publishing industry due to poorer quality books being produced—not the fault of the printer, I should add—it prevents wastage and storage fees for books that have been printed in advance, which may not be easy to sell.

Bookshops can frown on this method. Stores need to know they can easily return books (and gain stock for a reasonable price to begin with), and most POD platforms won't offer sale or return options to the author. However, be advised Ingramspark do, and they'll advise you what percentage is recommended, and how much returns may cost you.

Offset printing uses large rolls of paper and is used for most mass market paperback books because it offers higher quality and a wider variety of sizes. Usually, there is a minimum number of books you can order (for example, 50 in a batch). One of the great things, however, are the choices you're offered, such as gloss or matte cover finishes, embossing, varnishing, or even cloth-bound hardbacks. Lots of POD platforms will only offer gloss or matte finishes for paperbacks.

It sounds great, but it can be more expensive and an upfront investment is required to order in bulk. You'll need somewhere to store them, which means you're taking that extra risk.

Audio

When a book is read aloud as a recording—either by the author or a voice actor/actress—this is called an audiobook. They are great for people with less time and can be played through most devices. I know plenty of people who listen to them on the train to work or in the gym, and some even listen to them at a faster speed to increase the number of books they can enjoy a month.

One of the popular audiobook creation platforms is ACX, which is run by Amazon. You may also have heard of Audible or Findaway Voices. There are, however, plenty of others available for the creation and purchase of audiobooks.

If your book is being read in full, this will be the 'unabridged' version. If your book is being shortened, this will be the 'abridged' version.

Platform Comparisons

So, which is the best self-publishing platform? That's a difficult question and one I'm not going to answer. But I'm not going to leave you wondering about the options, either. I've used a variety of platforms and I think checking plenty out before you make a decision

Publishing Basics

is really important. If you're struggling to find the best platform for you, consider the following questions:

- Do they offer e-book options?
- Do they offer a variety of dimensions?
- Can you publish a hardback with them?
- Will they offer a free ISBN?
- Is it free to upload your files?
- Do they allow retailer returns?
- How easy is it to get in touch with them?
- Do they allow you to set a retailer discount?
- Can you give the book away for free?
- Do you get a choice of finishes/papers?
- How fast is the printing and shipping?
- Is the printer based in your country?
- Are they well known?
- How expensive is the process overall?
- Can you privately publish your book?

When you have some time, set up an account with a few of the companies and explore their systems in-depth. At this stage, you don't need to complete any of the payment or set-up details, but you can still access their help pages and tools to familiarise yourself. Be aware that each platform's features and prices may change, but research should give you an overview before you decide which one to use.

Why not begin a publishing journal and keep notes on what you want, and the companies that offer those things? You could start a page per company, or create a chart that ticks off all the things you want or need so you can easily compare.

Private Publishing

"I just want to publish the book so friends and family can read it. I'm not bothered about making money right now."

Sometimes we may just want to self-publish a book that only *we* have access to. Perhaps it's a family project or a personal journal you'd like to see in print, but don't want to make available for others to purchase. That's where private publishing applies, and most POD platforms will allow you to do this.

If you change your mind later, there is usually an option to allow distribution for that particular book and set a price at a later date. It may depend on the size and type of book, but if it's a standard fiction paperback in a 5x8" or 6x9", you should be good to go.

Note, however, that at the time of writing this, KDP does not currently offer this feature unless you are happy to receive books marked 'not for resale' on the cover. Such copies are great if you're passing them on for whatever reason (as it discourages unwanted re-sales). This might be for friends and family to see or for somebody to proofread, for example.

In Summary...

I've probably overwhelmed and terrified you already, but I'm going to continue nevertheless.

Please don't give up just yet, because in the next

chapter, we'll discuss some options and issues with self-publishing.

And *that's* where it gets interesting.

Step Two - Platform Considerations

In this chapter, I'll walk you through a few of my favourite platforms and some of the optional considerations available to authors through them, including returns, discounts and freebies. Let's start by looking at a great e-book platform.

Draft2Digital

Draft2Digital (D2D) is a digital publishing company that allows you to upload and self-publish an e-book. Their system is quick and easy to use, and they have clear reporting to display your sales data. Their handy formatting tools make it easy to create a free interior file, which you can download and export as either a PDF, MOBI, or an EPUB file to use in an e-book or a paperback. This means you can use their system to create an interior file and take it elsewhere if necessary.

But those file terms may not mean anything to you yet, so here's what they mean:

- **EPUB** – E-book file format
- **MOBI** – E-book file format (note that these will no longer be accepted on KDP from March

2025).
- **PDF** – 'Portable Document Format'
- **DOC** – Word Document

D2D's system also allows you to publish to a variety of platforms at the same time, and they act as a hub for all your sales data; they'll distribute your book to various companies such as Kobo, Nook, Apple and others for listings through those websites, increasing your reach. They also distribute to Amazon KDP (just be sure you haven't already published that same book with KDP to avoid duplication). They are now also able to help you with physical copies of your books.

Another great thing about D2D is you can set a zero price, meaning you can give it away free of charge. Although, D2D can distribute to Amazon KDP, and you'll have to set a price of 99p or above for that platform (as they require a minimum price).

Free Books

A brief note about free books, because I know a lot of you will get asked about free copies from friends, family and colleagues. Some of you may be publishing your book for this purpose alone.

First of all, know that **you are well within your rights to say no to giving your book away for free**—you'll be less likely to be a starving artist. I've found that the more you offer your work and services for free, the more people expect this of you in the long-run. When you start charging, you will lose followers and

Publishing Basics

readers—those who were only there to take advantage of your charity.

Charging for a book or an e-book is no different than charging for a cup of coffee in a café. They make the drink and you pay to consume it. The author creates the story and the reader pays to enjoy it. So if you want to charge for your book, then charge. This is business at the end of the day.

I tend to set a minimum price of 99p for an e-book, especially if it's the first in a series (because it will act as a hook).

Here are some ways to list your book at a zero price with Amazon, plus some pros and cons, because Amazon usually require a minimum price to be set.

- Publish the book with a zero price everywhere else (see Draft2Digital), then ask Amazon to match the price. You can contact Amazon through your KDP account. Alternatively, on the Amazon product page, you can click 'tell us about a lower price' and submit this way. Be patient as it may be a while for this to take effect, and remember that they do not have to agree to it.
- Run a KDP promotion if you are exclusive to Amazon's platform—they have some great countdown and free giveaway options. You can give your book away for up to 5 days every 90 days.

But if you don't want to use Amazon, you can always

consider the following:
- Use Draft2Digital, where setting a zero price is acceptable and circulated across a variety of platforms.
- Send the book via e-mail to subscribers as a gift, but beware of the risks here.
- Make the book easily available as a PDF download on your website, but beware of the risks here also.

Free Promotions - Benefits

- **New readers can try your work without losing money**—it's risk-free, with no financial loss, and ideal for those who usually only read traditionally published books or have just purchased an e-reader.
- **Great for people going on holiday** who are browsing the free/discounted content.
- **Will more people download the book if they don't have to pay for it**, even if they don't read it straight away?
- **Less of a piracy temptation;** if they can download the book free, there is no reason to unlawfully acquire or distribute it.
- If they enjoyed the first book for free, they may be more likely to pay for the other books in a series. **Free books are a great way to hook the reader.**
- **You will have a shot at getting into the Amazon bestseller list** for free books in your

genre.
- **People may be more likely to leave a review** if they downloaded for free and it was awesome.

Free Promotions - Limitations

- **You won't earn royalties** for those downloads.
- **Your book will be easily identifiable as independently published** if it's free all the time.
- **People may download it and never read it.**
- **People may be less likely to download the book**—if the book is free or of a very low cost, does this suggest the quality is poor or the author is desperate? Think about how you react to seeing free e-books on Amazon and make some notes in your journal.

Overall, my advice is to offer a free book as a temporary promotion only. The more urgent the offer, the more likely readers are to want to grab it while they can.

Stocking Your book

If you'd like to see your book on one of the most popular platforms (for publishing and shopping) and showing 'in stock' or available for quick delivery, then Amazon KDP is a good place to start.

It's nice to imagine your book will be 'in stock' on

the virtual shelves, but if you're using a POD service, it may not always be readily available.

When you publish with KDP, Amazon will list your paperback as showing 'in stock' automatically because it has been published through their platform—one of the benefits of using KDP. Amazon platforms can communicate quickly with other Amazon platforms so you may find any changes you make or new books you publish take effect much faster.

However, when you publish with Ingramspark or other non-Amazon companies who distribute to Amazon, it's common for those paperback books to show something along the lines of either 'out of stock—we don't know if/when this will be available' or 'out of stock—delivery estimated [enter time here].' In this case, delivery can be months.

You may ask, *who is going to buy a book that won't arrive for several months (that's not a pre-order)?* Well... exactly.

When this happened to me, my instinct was to panic. Who would order a book they might never get? When I contacted Amazon, I learnt that once somebody placed an order (proving there was a demand for the book), it would change to show 'in stock' because their system would generate an order for a few copies with whichever printer I was using. It makes sense that if one person wants a copy, another might too. And that's what happened—panic over.

I have since discovered if the book sells well, Amazon may also order stock in advance so your book will show 'in stock', then they may offer discounts on those copies if they don't sell right away. I logged in to check my reviews one afternoon and saw Amazon were selling one of my books (usually £15.99) at £4.00 per copy. Of course, I freaked out and contacted them to find out what had happened, concerned I wouldn't receive royalties. I was quickly assured this wouldn't be the case.

They explained that as the book was selling well, Amazon decided to order copies (paying my publisher for them at the price I'd set and therefore paying me the expected royalties per book). As they had the copies, they were then able to sell those on at whatever price they liked, and they just happened to have a sale on.

Amazon offer indie books on Prime sometimes (which is free next-day delivery for those who pay for the subscription), so having stock also allows them to fulfil those orders faster.

So in summary:
- **Publish with KDP** to have your books showing 'in stock' all the time.
- If you publish with a company that distributes to Amazon, **placing an order for that book can prompt Amazon's system** to order more copies from the printer to keep 'in stock'.
- **Having books 'in stock' with Amazon means they can offer them on Prime** delivery and sell them at sale prices.
- If you own your ISBN (so have not accepted a free one from the platform you're using) **you can print with multiple platforms**.

There's a quick and easy possible solution to listing

your books 'in stock' with Amazon. All you need to do is place an order for the book on their website like a reader would, and regularly search for the book's keywords and the ISBN (International Standard Book Number) daily if you can, so the system registers there is a demand for it. It may take a while for the status of the stock to change, if it actually does (this is not guaranteed to work!). You can also search from different devices (your phone and your laptop, for example).

If you're not publishing with Amazon, the platform you're using will circulate your book's listing to retailer websites such as Barnes & Noble, Waterstones, Rakuten, Google etc. It's up to these platforms individually if they show your book as 'in stock/available' or not. Lots of them will recognise the book is independently published and, therefore, will estimate a lengthy delivery to allow for printing and shipping.

At the end of the day, if they don't list your book as 'in stock' and you've tried the above, there's not much else you can do about it (other than publish your book direct through your favourite platforms for a faster listing on their website/s).

Second Hand Books

Some authors see their books being sold 'second-hand—like new' and worry because they don't understand what this means. Being new to the publishing game (and that's exactly how it can feel sometimes, like a game), please don't be alarmed if this happens to you. Most of the time, the process is the same. Whoever is listing your books will have already ordered and paid for them before being able to advertise them (therefore showing them as second-hand).

In short, don't worry. They may not have been pre-owned as such, but simply gone through an extra pair of hands before they reach the reader.

Of course, there is always the possibility the book is genuinely second-hand, which you won't earn royalties for. But still, that's pretty cool too, right?

Book Reviews

If your books are on Amazon, you can be confident readers have easy access to the review facilities. Note, however, that some customers who are new to Amazon and have not spent over a certain value may not be able to review products until they do.

But getting those who have the access to leave one can sometimes feel like you're fighting a losing battle. No matter how many times you ask a reader to leave feedback, sometimes they just won't. It's one of the things you can't control no matter how many times you try.

Then, of course, the reviews that *do* appear aren't always going to be positive. It can be heartbreaking for a writer to hear negative feedback, but either way, you need to hear it.

There are a few things you can do to increase the odds of receiving a review (positive or negative).

Firstly, include a link in the back of the e-book,

plus a list of your social media handles and website address. If it's right there and just a single click away, it's more tempting. You can also include a 'thank you' page, explaining how readers can support you further if they enjoyed the book. Some platforms will reject a book if it references a competitor's details, so it might be worth re-wording it a little.

You may also want to submit your book to Readers' Favorite for the chance to receive a free, honest review and a seal for the cover at readersfavorite.com if they award you with 5*. This can take a while, and the book is not guaranteed to be selected. If it isn't, you'll receive an email from them after a few months.

It never hurts to put a friendly reminder on social media and in newsletters. Ask your followers or Facebook friends to leave some honest feedback if they have read your book. Explain how reviews help independent authors and what their comments can help you achieve. Reviews let you know if you're on the right track, especially if you're writing a sequel. They help to convince other readers to buy the book. **I believe in quality, not quantity**; I'd be more likely to buy a book with five reviews all voting 4-5* than I would a book with 20 reviews, all 2-3*. Every reader is different, though, and I can't speak for them.

Reviews show the book has been/is being read. They make the book look and sound popular, particularly if the comments are all 'verified purchases'. And, of course, positive reviews make the author smile! A 'verified purchase' is a tag that will be attached to a review on Amazon when they can confirm the book was actually purchased through them. If somebody buys a book in Waterstones and leaves a review on Amazon, this tag will not be visible.

Consider sending out an advanced reader copy (ARC) before the book is out and ask those receiving them to review the book on its release day. Similarly, ask your BETA readers to leave reviews (more on BETA readers later). Some platforms allow readers to attach photographs of the book they have received, too, and some may require the reader to leave a short disclaimer to say they received the item free in exchange for their opinion. It's really important that you *do not* ask for only positive reviews, or give any incentives/payments for them (like 'review my book with 5* and I'll give you a £20 gift card). A reader should be making the decision to review the book on their own, and it should be 100% honest.

As we discussed in the previous section, give the book away for free for a short period; if people love the book and didn't have to pay anything for it, they might be more likely to leave you some positive feedback. This could also go the other way, though, because if they paid £9.99 for a book and hated it, are they more likely to be annoyed at their loss and leave a disgruntled review?

Occasionally, you may find Amazon remove or delete reviews if they believe them to be fake or posted by someone you know. They rightly do this to ensure all reviews are 100% honest and authentic, so potential buyers can make the best choices. If you share a surname or an address with the reviewer, this might be the cause of the problem.

Amazon isn't the only platform where readers can leave reviews, though. Most retailer websites now allow comments and star ratings. Goodreads is a community filled with book lovers looking to connect, review and challenge themselves. You'll find plenty of reviews there.

50 Reviews = Success?

I was once told that because my books (at the time) did not have many reviews—despite those it did have being 4-5* and extremely positive—that I *couldn't* be a successful self-publishing coach. My lack of reviews 'proved how poor my writing must be'. I can't roll my eyes here, but as I write this know that I'm rolling them.

This was a comment added to a Facebook feed where I'd offered a struggling author some help. It got me thinking. Despite all your efforts, you can *never* control the actions of your readers no matter how hard you try, and do we consider a book successful if it has tons of reviews? How many reviews should we be getting? I've seen 50 given as a guideline before.

In my experience, even if a reader thinks your book is incredible, there is *no way* to force them to leave a review. All we can do is politely ask and make the process as easy and as fast as possible. By constantly reminding and harassing them, you'll quickly lose their custom and will probably never get the review you wanted in the first place.

It's impossible to judge the quality and popularity of a book based solely on the number of

reviews it has. Comments and star ratings are super helpful at doing just that and more reviews do evidence more readers, but even *those* books are probably still missing hundreds of potential reviews, as are the bestsellers.

You may wish to make a list of what your initial opinions and reactions are to some books on Amazon that have a low number of reviews, or reviews with a low overall star rating.

Leaving Reviews

If you're unsure how to leave a review on Amazon, follow three simple steps. Find the book, sign in to your account, and then leave the review.

1. Find the book on Amazon and scroll to the bottom of the product page where the other reviews are displayed. On the left-hand side, there will be a button labelled 'write a customer review' beneath the heading, 'review this product'.
2. You will be asked to sign in to your Amazon account. You can still review the book on Amazon even if you did not purchase it there, but do leave a disclaimer to explain why if you can, and know it will not show as a 'verified purchase'.
3. Leave a star rating and complete the comments box. You can leave your review and even give it a title. Submit the review and within a few days, it should appear.

If you never leave reviews, it would be unfair to get upset if/when others don't leave them for you. I make a point of reviewing every book I finish, even if the book was terrible. If I don't finish it, however, I won't leave one because if I didn't read the whole thing, I can't realistically comment on the quality. However, I did review a book that disturbed me so much in the first half that I physically could not finish it, so I left a review to warn future readers that some of the content needed a disclaimer.

When I do have to leave a negative review, I always start by commenting on what I liked about the book first, then explain what I didn't like. I try to end on a positive if possible so the author doesn't take it personally. Like a positivity sandwich.

Put this book down and find something you've recently read by searching on Amazon (preferably indie, especially if it doesn't have very many at the moment). Go ahead and leave a review. You can even review *this* book if you've read enough of it or read it before.

Review Rules

Verified purchases can be confusing to new indie authors. If a reader buys your book through the Amazon platform and then leaves a review, *that* review will have a green 'verified purchase' stamp to indicate to other buyers that Amazon did sell that person your book (therefore, it's likely to be genuine), like a sales confirmation.

However, just because a review does not have this marker does not necessarily mean it's not genuine. Lots of people (myself included) who use Amazon a lot will review there regardless of where they bought it. Also, despite it going against Amazon's policies, some authors do still pay for reviews. By reimbursing whomever purchased and read the book, this will generate a 'verified purchase' label.

It's up to you to judge how valuable feedback is. In a nutshell, remember to stick to the rules.

People you are close to or who share the same address with you should not leave a review. They can always tell you what they thought in person, though, but platforms like Amazon may think these reviews are false and therefore remove them.

Never post or request false reviews; the comments and star ratings should be an accurate reflection of the buyers' opinions and **keep all reviews free from offensive language**. Lots of authors refuse to read their reviews whereas others rely on them for feedback—**review other books the way you would want people to review your own, with kindness and consideration.** Even if you did not enjoy a book, you can still be polite and reasonable. Provide constructive criticism, not cruel insults. Never pay someone to review your book as they will feel obliged to leave positive feedback and it will, as I mentioned above, cheat the system.

Be cautious when using any services and subscription platforms for reviews like pubby.co that allow authors to increase their reviews on Amazon, because on the surface, some do appear to break a few rules. However, when I did some digging, the one I tried *did* follow Amazon's guidelines and policies, mainly because no two authors could ever 'exchange' a review directly—you are not swapping reviews, but reading other books you think look good in exchange for points. You can then cash those points in whenever you're ready to ask other authors to read yours if they think it sounds good. The bigger the book, the more points you gain.

There is no way to choose who will review the book (and no way to guarantee it will actually be chosen). When you tell the platform about the book, **keep the information you input minimal.** I found lots of the readers selecting my novel when I tried one of these platforms were simply copying what I had written to create their review, using all my key descriptive words and unique aspects almost word-for-word. I reported these because, in my opinion, they had not actually read the book or they would have something more personal and specific to say about it. These seemed fake, so I had them removed. The less you tell them up front, the less likely they are to use it. Similarly, **report any reviews that seem AI generated** and be sure to explain why you believe they are. These can be removed, as can any reviews that are fake or incorrect. If they mention things that don't happen (such as characters that are not yours), flag them as it may be an error.

Any books you do select to review, be sure to read it cover-to-cover and leave at least one paragraph of honest and constructive feedback. Let the author know it's real by mentioning things you loved about the story, or your favourite characters. **Don't select books to review that you know you don't have time to read,** and when you have read a book, make sure you don't review it immediately as this may look suspicious. For low-content books, leave it until the next day if you can.

BETA readers or readers who receive ARCs (Advanced Reader Copies) can state this in their review if the platform requires it. For example, include a line that reads, 'I received this book free of charge in advance of its release in exchange for an honest review.' If you did not buy the book on Amazon but would like to leave a review there, the same may apply. A short disclaimer to state, 'I purchased this book elsewhere but like to leave reviews on Amazon' is helpful, but Amazon may still choose to remove it—the reviewer may also have had to spend a certain amount through the website before a review can be posted.

If you're the author rather than the reader and you use KDP, you can **add endorsements and reviews you have received externally to the product description** so these are automatically included for people to read. If you can get any public figures such as radio personalities or celebrities, popular social media influencers or other authors to review the book, this is where those comments would go. You can also use HTML codes to brighten the description, including adding bold, italic and underlined text in this section so they stand out a bit. You can Google 'Amazon supported HTML codes' or check their help section.

Discounting Your Book

A **wholesale discount** is how much of your book's retail price you give to the wholesaler/distributor and retailer. If you use a company such as Ingramspark, you can elect your own. Typically, the more you offer, the wider your distribution may be.

55-50% is fairly standard, and offering this means most stores can safely order the book, sell it at a discounted price and still make money. But, you're giving away half (or more) of your profit here, which for some authors is far too much. It was for me.

At 40%, most chain stores can comfortably stock the book. If you're targetting online sales, offering 40% won't alienate anyone. Most chain book stores will ask for 40% of royalties from sales anyway, whereas independent stores might ask for 30-35%. Anything less than this and you'd be looking at online sales only, or smaller high street shops.

Most independent publishing platforms such as Ingramspark will automatically calculate your royalties for you when you enter your book's price and the discount you've selected. These estimates make it easier to see if you'll be in profit and if so, by how much. Then you can decide if you want to increase or decrease that percentage based on what your aims are.

It may be worth noting, though, that in my experience some larger chain stores may already have a percentage agreed with the printer anyway, which means there is no need to offer such a high figure for the sake of one or two specific stores.

If your gut instinct is saying the percentage you're setting is too much, then feel free to lower it a little. Ingramspark will let you know what the minimums allowed for each territory are anyway.

Accepting Returns

Enabling returns allows book stores who may have ordered too much stock to send any unsold copies back. It's less of a risk for them to order in the first place, making the books more appealing. But it means we run the risk of losing money as the author because when those returns arrive back, we are charged.

With Ingramspark, you can opt to have books returned to *you* if stores do send them back (for a small fee) or you can have them destroyed. Alternatively, you can switch off returns altogether. If you switch them off at a later date, stores then have a time limit to return unwanted copies before they are no longer accepted.

Pre-Orders

While you're promoting the upcoming release date for your book, wouldn't it be great if readers could order and pay for the book in advance? Pre-orders do exactly this—the book is available for readers to purchase online, claiming their copy early so they don't forget to do so later on.

You're not as popular as the big names yet, so every sale at this stage counts. If you're telling someone about the book you're releasing next month, are they likely to remember everything when the book finally releases? Will they have lost that scrap of paper you wrote your details on? Have they been out and bought from another author in the meantime? Are they even still interested?

Setting up pre-orders at least a month in advance means any promoting you do beforehand isn't wasted. If you can set up a pre-order sooner, it's a good idea.

Some platforms will expect you to upload the finalised product around 7 business days in advance of the release date. They need to be sure what readers are paying for is the finished book. They'll likely send you an email and ask you to check the version they have, then approve it for sale. They may then temporarily prevent access to that book through your account until release day, or if you miss the deadline, you'll be asked to wait a while before they allow you to arrange any pre-orders again.

Step Three - Things You Should Know

Distributors & Wholesalers

You may also be curious about distributors and wholesalers, and what the difference is between the two. These are terms you will come across regularly. Manufacturers (so in our circumstances this would be the printer) deal with distributors, and distributors deal with wholesalers.

Manufacturer → Distributor → Wholesaler

A distributor handles orders and holds the stock. They're unlikely to deal directly with the customer due to the size and quantity of the stock they hold, and *that's* where wholesalers come in. They do, sometimes, also sell to retailers direct, however.

A wholesaler will buy from the distributor and sell on terms that have been agreed with a retailer. They'll often buy a large amount of stock (bulk buying) and then offer discounts on those products.

It can sometimes be confusing as some of the companies will do both, for example, Bertrams and Gardeners. Companies such as Amazon, Waterstones and WHSmiths are booksellers, aka the retailers.

Copyright

Copyright protects your work from being copied and distributed without your permission, and in the UK there is no need to register this with the government.

From creation, a manuscript is protected for the life of the author, plus 70 years. To read more about UK copyright, please visit: gov.uk/copyright.

To show your work has been copyrighted, you will need to include a line to state this in the book itself.

Here are two examples of how you can format this:

1. *Copyright 2025 Rachael Hardcastle*
2. *© 2025 Rachael Hardcastle*

To insert the copyright symbol in a document, you can press Alt 0169 as a shortcut or access the symbol through your computer's character map.

You can download free copyright page templates online fairly easily. Alternatively, open up a book you own and check out how they've structured this page.

Copyright in the US works differently. As a general rule, it is usually for the life of the author plus 70 years, though there are other factors to consider. Authors can also submit a form to copyright their material with the United States Copyright Office.

First Editions

A first edition is a term used to describe the first 'version' of your book. You should publish a new edition if you make significant changes to the book's content, such as adding or removing sections. You may have seen 'revised' editions before.

If you produce a book with large print or that is Dyslexia friendly, this would count as a new edition, and so would a hardback.

Be aware that different platforms may describe editions differently; their requirements for a new edition and therefore a new ISBN may vary, and you don't always need a new edition if you change the cover.

Generally, if you're just amending the odd spelling or typing error, you don't need to begin a new edition, either. It would need to include a significant change (a new introduction or an extra chapter) for example.

International Standard Book Number (ISBN)

An ISBN is 10-13 digits long and can be found on the back of the book near the barcode. On Amazon, you may have noticed products also have an ASIN, including e-books. This stands for 'Amazon Standard Identification Number'.

As an independent publisher, I'm frequently asked 'should I buy my own ISBN?' and the answer to this question is yes, which is probably not what you want to hear. While free ISBNs are handy and will save you money they, unfortunately, offer more limitations than benefits.

When you use a free ISBN, that platform is listed as the publisher of the book. Find a self-published book on Amazon and scroll down to read through the details. Where it states 'publisher', you will notice a POD company is named rather than the author. By purchasing your ISBN, you can not only list yourself as the publisher of the book if that's what you want, but you could also enter the details of your own self-publishing company if you have one.

Think about this from a book store's point of view. Most large chain stores will not want to give their money to a competitor so are less likely to order copies of the book if that competitor is listed as the publisher. Amazon is a big competitor when it comes to books.

Although it still doesn't look as impressive as it would if the publisher shown was one of the big five, listing an independent or small press rather than your name or a competitor means stores may be more likely to order shelf stock. As awkward as it sounds (because I'm sure you are proud of your self-publishing status), it helps to mask that you're not using a well-known publishing house.

Alternatively, you can use your ISBNs for paperbacks and hardbacks only. I use Draft2Digital and KDP for e-books and you can take advantage of the free ISBNs they offer. You can download the Kindle Create programme to your desktop, which allows you to quickly and easily design the interior of your e-book by uploading the paperback document you already have. It's free to download and use.

Once you've used a variety of their tools and it

looks the way you want, you can export the e-book in a Kindle format to make uploading to KDP less of a chore. You can download Kindle Create* from Amazon, or simply type it into Google.

By doing this, you can reserve your expensive ISBNs for physical books. And don't worry, Amazon allows you to enter the name of the publisher and will then link the two formats together so your readers can shop conveniently. If this doesn't happen automatically, send them an e-mail and ask. The only downside to doing the above (using one platform for paperbacks and one for digital) is rather than having one dashboard to check for sales and royalty platforms, you might have two or three. For example KDP and D2D.

Another benefit of using your own ISBN is having access to the details publishers, distributors and potential customers see when they search for your book. If you live in the UK, you'll purchase your ISBN through Nielsen. They ask that you then register with their Title Editor to access your book's listing. Be aware that it can take a few weeks to receive your login information, but once you do, it's a handy tool to have.

*Kindle Create offers 3 options. One is a print replica (exactly the same interior as your paperback or hardback print book). It will be a fixed PDF layout.

They also offer the ability to create comics, letting the reader zoom.

Finally, you can create a reflowable document for books like novels or memoirs. The text and fonts can be adjusted and it will adapt to the device your reader is using.

Nielsen Title Editor

Nielsen Title Editor allows the author/publisher to manage their book's data on the database. This includes the title, subtitle, series, ISBN, website, contributors, languages, audiences, reviews and awards, the book cover and more. You can also list the prices and if the book is returnable etc.

The information on Title Editor will override any information supplied by the printing platform you're using. So if you publish through KDP and do not set up anything on Nielsen, retailers will see what you entered on KDP. If you do set up on Nielsen, the data you input there will be what retailers see.

It is currently a free service to use, though you can pay for an enhanced service if you wish.

nielsentitleeditor.com/titleeditor
nielsenbook.co.uk/isbn-agency

Legal Deposits

Something few independent authors in the UK realise is that they are legally required to submit one copy (the most up to date edition/version of their book) to the British Library for cataloguing within one month of publication at the author's/publisher's cost.

You should send your book via recorded mail, preferably so somebody has to sign for it and allow plenty of time for them to confirm receipt. It's always a good idea to have a record of the book being sent and

Publishing Basics

safely received. It may take a short while for you to receive an acknowledgement, but a letter or email will eventually be sent to thank you. If you're using a PO Box, be sure to check it regularly to avoid missing updates.

If you do not send a book or you forget, you may receive an email from them politely asking that you fulfil this. You may also receive reminders.

If you're publishing something different such as a magazine or a pamphlet, you may still need to submit. You can visit their website at bl.uk for guidelines and further information, including their address.

Also, know that other libraries in the UK can request further copies of your work up to 12 months after its release and if this happens, the same rule applies. You must send these at your own cost within one month of the request, and generally the request will be for five copies.

You should never assume that your self-publishing platform is sending these on your behalf (they may very well be doing this, but they are unlikely to notify you if/when they do).

The other libraries are as follows:
- Bodleian Libraries University of Oxford
- Cambridge University Library
- The National Library of Scotland
- The National Library of Wales
- The Library of Trinity College Dublin

Category Codes

When you publish a book, you will be asked to select the most relevant categories. For example, you may select Fiction as a general category, then sub-categories of Young Adult and Fantasy. The general advice is to select no more than three. See BISAC (Book Industry Standards and Communication bisg.org/page/BISACEdition) as an example, which is a standard list used by US and English-speaking companies to properly shelve your work at the retailer level.

You wouldn't want your erotic vampire novel being wrongly shelved in middle-grade children's fiction. That's why it's so important to correctly 'label' your book and its genre so it can be ideally placed for your target audience.

Different platforms may use different cataloguing processes, so follow their drop down options to see what their listings are.

Step Four - Take Care of Yourself

Public Liability Insurance

If a third party is injured or something of theirs is damaged while you're at an event or during their visit to your premises, public liability insurance will cover the cost of any legal action and/or compensation claims they may make.

Most authors have banners up, displayed proudly so passers-by know who they are. But what if one of those fell over? How are you going to pay any fees? That's where PLI comes in.

Professional Indemnity

Professional indemnity insurance will generally cover any claims against you or your company which arise from alleged (or actual) breaches of your duty as a professional. If you offer services to others, this is something you may wish to consider. If clients claim for compensation or if you are sued for a financial loss caused by your service, this would be relevant.

If you do offer services to others, you must protect yourself (and your clients) by using a contract and a waiver of liability. Services such as copy-editing are subjective and different editors will do things in different ways—what is acceptable to one may not be acceptable to another, and authors should know ahead of time that as editors are only human, sometimes errors do slip through.

As a professional, ask that your clients read and sign to agree to a contract, which shows they fully understand well in advance what any risks may be. You should, wherever possible, gain a wet signature rather than an electronic one.

I'm not a lawyer or an insurance specialist so please consult a professional.

Journaling

Other than an excuse to buy a gorgeous journal and a snazzy new pen to write with, personal/private journaling has some amazing benefits.

Writing is a solitary hobby and an even lonelier business if you're running it solo. There are some things you just can't discuss with friends and family; petty complaints you have or self-pity you're feeling (all of which is normal and perfectly OK, by the way), so it's nice to have a safe, private space where you can dump all this without fear of what others will think.

It's like free self-therapy, and I wouldn't be without mine. I used to journal every night before bed, but due to my busy schedule, I now journal only when I feel I need to. If things get too much—if I have a particularly rough day or come across someone who made my blood boil—I write it down. Then I'm not going to sleep feeling anxious, upset or angry.

You may be wondering why I bothered to include a journaling section in a book about self-publishing. As an author, the public needs to see the best of you at all times; you should be setting a positive example for your company, fellow indie authors, and your readers. People need to feel comfortable talking to you, so being approachable and offering a pleasant smile is a must at an event. If you're worried or stressed, without realising, this can sometimes show in your body language and the way you interact with people. You will seem less invested and interested in what that person has to say because internally, you're worrying about something unrelated. We all have bad days. You're not expected to be at your best 100% of the time, but your sales will suffer if you don't put in the effort.

Journaling is a great way to empty your mind before and after an event. I'm sure you'll meet people who inspired you, but you may also meet people who grind your bones. By writing this down, you're taking an easy step to being in the ideal frame of mind both during and after your book signing.

Some writers keep a voice journal and record their thoughts on a dictation machine (or an app on their phone) and some express themselves through art. Your method is your own—there are no right or wrong ways to journal.

Success Journal

When I first started taking myself seriously as an *authorpreneur* (an author/entrepreneur—it's a thing), I religiously checked my social media following every day and, in my 'success journal', noted down my progress to keep track of the increase/decrease, and linking this to promotions or events. Whilst this was good business sense (because we *do* need to know if the advertisements we're paying for are working) it became addictive (like most social media can be).

From 2016, I kept what I called a 'success journal' and completed this every day in a page-a-day format. But, I soon became obsessed with checking the figures, relying purely on numbers to satisfy my need to be 'successful'—if I lost a single follower, I panicked, wondering what I'd done wrong and who they were. **Did their lack of support make me feel any less of an author?** Sometimes it did. So, at the end of 2018, I decided to stop and note down my thoughts, feelings and observations as part of my regular personal journaling time. Once a week, I'd check social media to ensure nothing dramatic had changed and any promotions or posts I did share were working, then simply added a few lines to my personal journal entry.

These days, I'm so busy that I don't have time to worry about numbers on a social media page. I post what I need to, when I need to, and any increase in that number at the end of the month is a lovely bonus. Even then, I don't always check them. It's nice if people want to follow me on socials, but it doesn't affect my

Publishing Basics

mindset now when they don't.

Try not to worry or obsess over the number of followers, fans, and likes you have in general. You can hide these figures on the platforms that allow it, because at the end of the day, they do not accurately reflect your success. YouTube is a great example; you can access the figures should you need them, but they are not publicly displayed.

A personal journal is a 'dear diary' style of journaling, where there is no pressure to write anything in particular or anything at all; the words can flow for as long as they need to and as honestly as you like. Only you will ever see it. It's a place to discuss friends, family, work and other non-business or author-related topics. Scribble, draw and scrapbook. You can complete this as often as you like.

A success journal is a diary purely business-related; a place to keep track of your platforms, express any worries, calculate expenses etc. A safe, private place for you to empty your mind of all things author/success/business-related. Complete this weekly if you can, but don't worry if you need to walk away. Because the trick to sticking to a success journal is making it fun and interesting—you should *want* to write in it. You can use heart or star-shaped Post-It notes when someone compliments you or your book/s (or provides positive feedback in any way), so on the days you're feeling down, you can flick back and read all the wonderful things people had to say.

Keep track of your sales using a tally, but don't feel bad if those numbers aren't high. Sales can fluctuate for numerous reasons including factors you can't control, which we will talk about in the marketing section. But, by keeping this tally for a full year, you can assess which months were more successful for you and thereby (hopefully) why that was. For example, gifts purchased for Christmas in December.

If you must track a social media platform's growth, focus only on two at a time. I used to track Facebook and Twitter—this bit gets addictive so try to avoid checking more than once per week. If you use a bullet journal*, you're probably already used to habit trackers and what they're all about.

The rest of your journaling space is for your private thoughts. It's also an ideal place to note down contact information for authors you meet, interviewers, reviewers, book store managers, bloggers, and anyone in the media.

*I'm not going to explain bullet journaling here, but if you're interested and would like to get creative, check out bulletjournal.com.

Positive Affirmations

If your book isn't selling as well as you hoped, it can feel disheartening and disappointing. As a sufferer of anxiety, I often use positive affirmations to re-focus my mind and control unwanted symptoms, so I wanted to share a short paragraph on affirmations with you because they can work equally as well when you're at an event or about to do a reading.

A positive affirmation is a completely positive

statement that you can say aloud or to yourself, which starts with the phrase 'I am' and is written in the present tense. Say them when you're feeling worried to help re-program thought patterns, therefore changing the way you feel. Positive affirmations do *not* replace taking action, though. Here are some affirmations examples:

*'I'm a confident writer who **doesn't** have to **worry** about **not** selling books.'*

'I am a confident, talented writer, capable of selling lots of books.'

The first example is incorrect as it includes negative words. In the second example, I have re-written that same sentence as a correct affirmation. If you have a notebook or a journal handy, give them a try.

PREPARATION

Step One - Editing

Hire An Editor

Yes, you need an editor. But I'm not going to tell you to *hire* one. This is where my advice differs from what you may hear most other writers say.

One of the main manuscript preparation subjects I often discuss with aspiring writers is editing, because it's overwhelming and expensive and often, they want to know how they can avoid all that. The short answer is that you can't, but there are ways around a huge bill.

Before you do anything (other than a re-write or reading the darn thing), you should research what a professional editor would do. Basically, they will look over both the technical issues in the book—for example, spelling and grammar—and the story itself, including character arcs* and subplots.

I wouldn't recommend editing your book solo. Even if you choose not to hire someone, your book must still be read and checked by *someone*—paid or otherwise—because you're too close to your own project to see it subjectively. As you're reading through each paragraph, your brain is already skipping ahead because you know your story, so an outside perspective is key. If you do decide to hire somebody, chat with a few editors beforehand; be sure you 'mesh' well and get along—you'll be working closely with this person to iron through something important to you. You need to build a professional, trusting relationship with them. But know that editors don't have to be qualified. They should, however, have a keen eye and, preferably, lots of experience. And also remember that it's subjective and they're only human—some errors do still slip through. I've seen my fair share in bestsellers so it's normal. Most will offer you a free sample so you can judge for yourself if they're the right fit for your book, and you may be able to pay in instalments. Look for someone with experience in your genre, too.

I started editing as a hobby because I found it was something (other than writing) that I was good at, so I took a course. Since then, I've worked freelance, gaining experience and finding regular clients. It's now a key part of my publishing business.

If you cannot afford to hire a professional, you could ask someone you know to help out. Somebody who works with text every day (an English teacher, for example) would be ideal. The quality of editing may affect the book's success, so you should never release anything before it has been thoroughly edited.

I always stick to my 'Six Read Rule' which I'll cover later.

*Character arcs are the inner journey (and/or physical journey) of a character and the completion of a lesson learnt. This is how the character develops and

Preparation

transforms throughout your story.

There are two types of editing to consider:

1. **Copy editing (sometimes written as copy-editing) aka line editing**, which looks at the consistency and accuracy of your manuscript, checking for spelling, grammar, and punctuation. This covers what I like to call the 'technical sh*t'.
2. **Developmental editing aka content editing**, which looks at improving the content and its structure. This may be the story, sub-plots, and the characters.

Editors may all offer different services, charging different prices and working in their own way. This is a subjective profession, so not all editors will fault the same things. What one identifies as an error, another may allow. And although editing can be expensive, it's worth hiring more than one if you can for that exact reason.

Editors can work with either a hard copy of the manuscript (on printed paper) or an electronic document. The latter is preferred because it's much easier and faster—they'll likely use the 'track changes' facility of their word processor. This way, the author can see what an editor has changed and why; both can leave and reply to comments, too.

Ideally, you would follow this path when it comes to the editing process: alpha reader → developmental editor → copy-editor → proofreader → BETA reader.

1. **Proofreaders** are usually hired once editors have done their job. They are the final professional defence against mistakes.
2. **ALPHA readers** are given access to early versions of the manuscript. Their feedback can help to develop the book in its beginning stages. Friends and family are often the first we think of and trust to read our work, but if they fear upsetting or offending us, will they be honest?
3. **BETA readers** are unpaid volunteers who will read the book for fun and identify any problems they come across. This can be anything from missed grammatical errors to unresolved sub-plots.

Lots of independent authors substitute editors and proofreaders with BETA readers alone, which is a mistake. It's always wise to get a second or third eye before your book goes anywhere near the public—your reputation is at stake, and you could anger a reader who paid good money for a book (and in good faith) if it's filled with lazy, unnecessary errors.

I rarely use alpha readers because I enjoy keeping the initial creation of my books private. But when I approach BETA readers, it's usually after the first copy-editing phase has been completed, when I've had a chance to complete my 'Six Read Rule'. I ask 10-15 different people for their thoughts, ensuring they are within my target audience. There would be no point asking avid science-fiction readers to comment on your romance novella. It wouldn't interest them. They may not know what to look for. If your book is aimed at both male and female readers, look for anyone with hobbies and reading preferences that are relevant to your genre (for example, children under the age of 12 who like dinosaurs).

Set some clear questions you'd like to be answered, including anything you're worried about. This might be the relationship between two characters or the way you kill the villain at the end. Ask your BETA readers to pay close attention to those areas of concern.

Book and Chapter Length

If you've asked yourself one of these questions recently, this short section is for you. I get asked this question almost every time I give a talk on creative writing.

- *Is my book the correct length?*
- *Are my chapters too short?*
- *Should I make this book a series?*

Books and chapters can be as long as they need to be. That's pretty much it. Ideally, a novel needs to be longer than 50,000 words, though some sit at approximately 40,000 and get away with it. Anything less than 70,000 words can be frowned upon, especially if you're writing for an adult.

Sometimes, the length of your book can depend on the genre you're writing and what your readers are expecting for their money. Generally, anything between 80,000-100,000 words is acceptable, but in high/epic fantasy and science-fiction, you can aim higher (100,000+). However, if you're target audience are younger, your word count should be lower to meet their needs and abilities.

Pre-school/picture books need only be around 500 words, but middle-grade fiction is perhaps 20,000-50,000 words. Chapter books would ideally also include some black and white illustrations, but not as a full-spread the way a toddler's picture book would be formatted.

Young adult (YA) fiction continues up to approximately 80,000 words.

There are, of course, different types of books to consider outside of genre. You may have heard of terms such as 'novella', 'novelette' and 'flash fiction'. I've found, generally, the lengths for these are as follows:

- **Picture Books** – up to 500 words
- **Flash Fiction** – up to 1,000 words
- **Short Story** – up to 7,000 words
- **Novelette** – up to 15,000 words
- **Novella** – up to 40,000 words
- **Novel** – up to 100,000+ words

These figures vary depending on your source, so try Googling the lengths of your favourite books or books in the genre you're writing for a better idea.

One book is called a stand-alone, but if you have

more than one planned, you're writing a series. Two is a duology. Three is a trilogy, and four is a quartet.

Rachael's Six Read Rule

As a copy-editor, it's important to catch as many mistakes in a manuscript as possible. However, authors should self-edit their work thoroughly before sending it to a professional, and that's where my 'Six Read Rule' comes in.

I've developed a strategy for new writers to help them cover as many issues from the below list as possible in just six rounds of edits. Each round looks at something different and preps the manuscript to then be read by somebody else.

Self-editing may not only reduce how long it will take for your professional editor to complete their part, but it may also help keep your costs down.

Between each of the following steps, put your manuscript away for 48 hours. By taking a short break from the text, not only can your eyes rest, but you may not grow so weary or bored of repeatedly reading the same thing.

Here is a break-down of my 'Six Read Rule':

1. **Plot and character (aka the developmental edit).** Before you do anything else, read your manuscript and be sure your setting, character arcs and motivations and storyline make sense, are full and complete, clear and concise. Once you have a rounded story, then move on to...

2. **Spelling and grammar.** This round of editing should include UK vs US spellings, homonyms, initial -ing words, pronouns, slang, types of speech, clichés, metaphors and so on. Cover as much of the 'technical sh*t' as you possibly can. You may wish to use some editing software for this stage, like ProWriting Aid. Once you're happy, then try...
3. **Punctuation and sentence length variation.** Check if your commas can be replaced with semi-colons or em dashes. Have you opened and closed all your speech marks/quotation marks and brackets? Do all your questions have question marks and all your sentences have periods? Also consider your tone, pacing and author's voice at this stage if you can. At this point, you can take a look at your...
4. **Formatting.** You can use Ctrl F to find and replace words in your document. This can aid with the removal of double spacing—you only need one space between a full stop and the capital letter of your next sentence, not two. At this stage, run through your dialogue and be sure you have formatted this correctly. If words are split at the end of a line with a hyphen, keep these to a maximum of four per page. After that, it's time to consider the...
5. **Accuracy**. Check your facts are correct and relevant. If you have references, ensure these are all noted and formatted well. If you're writing an e-book, do all your hyperlinks work? Finally, read it again for...

Preparation

6. **Entertainment value.** Read and check your manuscript from a reader's perspective rather than an editor's. Read it in various formats (for example: printed, on-screen, aloud). You could also read sections out of order or even backwards. Is the story entertaining? Are your characters relatable? Did you enjoy it?

The first chapter of your book is likely to need more work because it was the first thing you wrote (while still getting into the flow and feel of your voice). It's the first thing a reader will see both online and in the shop when they open and sample your book, so be sure to go through that several times. Poor editing in a sample or a 'look inside' feature via an online retailer like Amazon can instantly put a reader off purchasing a copy, so take extra care here.

Between finishing your first draft and self-editing your book, put the manuscript away and forget about it for a few weeks. When you return, you will have detached from the project and will see it in a new light. Perhaps also add a few weeks between each stage of the Six Read Rule for the same reason.

And remember, you're only human. Errors slip through. There may be a few in here. I guarantee as soon as I hit publish, I will turn to a random page and find something (because that's what always happens, you'll see!). If you've done your absolute best, that's all a reader can ask for.

*Technical Sh*t*

I mentioned above how copy-editing looks at the 'technical sh*t' in your manuscript. Or the 'boring sh*t' if you'd rather be writing. Personally, I rather enjoy picking fault and fixing things. The following list by no means includes everything, but it covers the main issues and can act as a checklist for you during the editing process.

- **Spelling**
- **Grammar**
- **Punctuation**
- **Repetition** such as unnecessary uses of the word 'that'.
- **Sentence Length Variation**
- **Redundancies** (aka tautology) are words that repeat the meaning of another word (saying the same thing twice/in two different ways).
- **Pacing**
- **Consistency**
- **Homonyms** are words that sound the same but are spelt differently. An example would be 'their', 'they're', 'there'.
- **Choice of Vocabulary**
- **Accuracy**
- **Clichés** are overused phrases. A good example would be, 'cold as ice'.
- **Similes and Metaphors.** In writing, when we say something is *like* something else, this would be a simile. If we say something *is* something

else, it's a metaphor.
- **Fillers** are overused words such as 'that', which can often be removed from sentences without changing the meaning.
- **Slang**
- **Tense** (past or present, for example)
- **Point of View** (first and third person, for example)
- **Types of speech** (noun, verb, adjective, adverb etc.)

I highly recommend you also research what you need to look for when self-editing your manuscript, particularly the various punctuation marks and how/when to use them.

One of the most frustrating ones is probably the em-dash (—). I'll break down a few others in the next section for you.

Types of Speech

A noun is a person, thing or place. Proper nouns are usually capitalised names, such as 'Rachael' or 'University of Imagination'. Common nouns do not need capitalising, such as 'apple'. A pronoun is a replacement for a name, so 'he' or 'she' would be an example.

A verb is an action such as 'walk'. An adverb changes the verb. *'Emma ran quickly up the stairs.'* In this example, 'quickly' is the adverb, 'ran' is the verb, and 'Emma' is the proper noun.

An adjective describes a noun or a pronoun, such as 'hairy'.

Punctuation Problems?

There are certain punctuation marks you may not use day-to-day, so don't worry if you're not familiar with some of these.

An em-dash (—) is the width of an 'm' and if often used to replace a comma. When using an em-dash, avoid adding spaces before and after as you would with other punctuation marks *'like—this'* rather than *'like — this'*. The em-dash can also replace parenthesis.

An en-dash (–) is the width of an 'n' and marks ranges or differences, for example, *'2-3'* or *'Leeds-London'*.

A hyphen (-) is the shortest of the three and is used to hyphenate words, such as *'three-dimensional'*.

You can use the handy keyboard shortcut Alt 0151 on your keyboard to insert an em-dash and Alt 0150 for an en-dash.

Parenthesis are also known as brackets and there are three types.

{ } which I call the 'curly ones' are used for sets. You would use them around numbers such as your times tables *'{3,6,9,12}'*.

( ) which are the 'normal ones' are those we use frequently. They add extra information to sentences, for example, *'(even though she promised she would)'*.

[ ] which I've named the 'square ones' are used

Preparation

around already bracketed items, such as in equations like '*[(2+2) + (3+5)]*'

Semi-colons (;) and colons (:) are used for different things but are often confused.

Colons are generally used for lists. '*I went to the store and bought: bananas, apples and pears.*' They can also be used to introduce something, '*He bought me the two things I wanted most of all: books and coffee.*'

Semi-colons join two sentences and can be used in place of commas or periods when each sentence could also stand on its own. They can be used to separate items in a list (if some of those items already contain commas).

A period (.) is just another word for a full stop.

Ellipsis (...) are three full stops together. You can use them when something is missing, for example, when words have been removed from a quote.

Here is a quick list of punctuation marks for you to reference as/when you need to:

Comma	,
Colon	:
Semi-Colons	;
Period/Full Stop	.
Speech Marks	"text"
Quotation Marks	'text'
Parentheses/Brackets	{} [] ()
Exclamation Mark	!

Question Mark	?
En-Dash	–
Em-Dash	—
Hyphen	-
Ellipsis	...

If you'd like to learn about self-editing, try downloading a programme such as Grammarly (which is free with the option to upgrade) and have a read through the errors it highlights in your manuscript. The website is grammarly.com. Alternatively, try Autocrit at autocrit.com, which is how I started, or ProWriting Aid at prowritingaid.com.

Why not include a round of editing using the above software as part of your routine?

Tense & Point of View (POV)

Tense and POV can be tricky, particularly if you switch from one to the other during your story. Be sure these are consistent and that any changes (hopefully done with purpose) are clear.

When writing in first person, your text is written from your character's point of view, as if they are telling the story. They would use 'I' a lot, for example, '*I went to the shop.*' This can be limiting as a writer, as you can only tell the reader what is going on in the main character's (aka the protagonist's) mind.

Second person, however, is where the writer talks to the reader. They will say things like '*you walk to the shop.*' This is used much less often.

In third person, that same sentence might say, '*She*

went to the shop', so the author tells the reader about a third party. This provides some additional options as the writer can share what other characters are thinking, such as the villain (aka the antagonist).

Tense is easier to understand. '*I went to the shop*' is past tense, because you're explaining what has already happened. '*I am going to the shop*' is present tense because it's happening now, whereas '*I will go to the shop*' is future tense because it hasn't happened yet. If you get stuck, use this quick reminder:

- First - I
- Second – You
- Third – They
- Past – did
- Present – doing
- Future – will do

Active Vs Passive Voice

The best way to explain active and passive voice is by demonstrating it. It's the difference between somebody doing something, or the something being done by the person. Here is an example:

Active: 'Rachael ate a pizza for dinner.'
Passive: 'For dinner, the pizza was eaten by Rachael.'

Passive voice can weaken your text, though you don't need to avoid using it completely.

In the active example, Rachael is eating the pizza whereas, in the passive example, the pizza is being eaten by Rachael.

Front and Back Matter

Front matter refers to everything at the front of the book before the story begins. This may include the title pages, 'also by' page (if you have written any other books or want to list the order of the books in the series), the author's dedication, ISBN/copyright information and so on.

Back matter refers to everything at the back of the book after the story finishes. This may include the 'author's note', or the 'about the author' section (if you choose to include one), indexes, references and so on.

Although this material is not technically part of the novel, it will still need to be edited and proofread as typing errors may exist there.

Also, be sure to check any poems you include throughout, other material such as images (if they include any text), maps, diagrams, and anything else additional to the chapters themselves.

Step Two - Formatting

Formatting is Easy?

First thing's first: the advice in this section is based on Open Office (OO) because it's free and does the same things most other word processors do. If you're just starting and haven't paid for Microsoft Word, try OO. If you've been writing a while, you might be already using Microsoft Word. Please note that the tools may be in different locations or work in a slightly different way to OO, but the same options should be available. Both systems work well with each other as they are compatible.

Although there are an abundance of forums, blogs, and videos to help you to format your manuscript, when you're completely new to the process it can be overwhelming attempting to sift and sort through everything.

When I first started as an indie author, I wanted to learn how to do things myself so I had a working knowledge, plus save some cash along the way. I also wanted to know in advance of outsourcing what the job entailed (so I would know if someone tried to rip me off!). Some authors simply aren't interested and like to outsource (hire somebody) to format for them. I'm going to assume in this chapter that you'd like to learn some basics (or else why include it in the book?).

What you will need to do first and foremost is check what your publisher's/printer's specifications are. You then have to format to those requirements. This information can be found on their website, usually as a PDF you can download. Some of them may even give you a template to use, which is even better. Occasionally, you'll find a handy chart that breaks down the dimensions of the book based on the paper quality you choose, with and without bleed.

You can download and install OO quickly, easily and free of charge. openoffice.org is their website. Alternatively, if you're looking for more in-depth software, you can purchase and download Scrivener, which is not only great for writing and planning your book, but also for formatting and exporting in a suitable style. Visit literatureandlatte.com for more information.

Creating Page Styles

Although it can be a pain, it'll save you tons of time and stress later if you set up some page styles in advance. Page styles are types of pages that you preset before you begin. In OO, you can create these through 'Styles and Formatting', then by selecting 'Page Styles'.

I recommend you set up two different page styles to begin with. Name one 'Normal' and the other 'Plain'. Or 'Basic' and 'Blank'. To do this, right-click on the 'Page Styles' toolbar and select 'new'.

Preparation

The plain style is self-explanatory; we'll use this on pages where you need nothing but empty space—it's going to be plain/blank. This style won't even include page numbers, headers or footers. When you start a new chapter on the right-hand page, often on the left you'll see there is a completely blank one.

So, the normal style is for all your other pages (if you're writing fiction). If you're writing non-fiction, you might want to set up a page style per chapter, because this will then allow you to apply a different header and footer for each topic (like you see in this book). If you decide to do it, name your styles after the chapters because it makes life easier.

Once you've named your first style, you'll need to set up your page for that style. And before you do anything else, select the size of the book. Some of the more popular **dimensions** are:

- 5x8"   Fiction/Non-Fiction/Poetry
- 6x9"   Fiction/Non-Fiction/Hardback
- 8x10"   Children's Picture Book
- 4.25"x7"   Pocket Size Fiction/Poetry

My book *To See A World* is a 5"x8", whereas *Noah Finn & the Art of Suicide* is a 4.25"x7". There are a variety of options available, though; check with your printer as some platforms may not offer the full range.

Next, you'll need to set the margins. Pick up the nearest book to you and naturally open to any spread. Take note of how you hold the book—the placement of your thumbs, how wide you open it, the text's proximity to the spine.

I usually set my margins to 2cm (inner) then 1.27cm for the others in the list (outer, top, bottom), which is how this book is formatted. This is because I want to ensure the inside text is easy to read without having to bend the spine. I also like to leave the reader space at the outer edges to rest their thumbs without covering any words.

- Inner: 2cm
- Outer: 1.27cm
- Top: 1.27cm
- Bottom: 1.27cm

Select a portrait or landscape orientation depending on the book you're producing, then choose a 'mirrored' page layout. Portrait means the book will be taller rather than wider and landscape layouts are wider and shorter. Everything else in that set-up section can be ignored.

- Portrait for fiction
- Mirrored (you want the left and right pages to mirror each other, so the same settings apply.)

Once you're happy, you can move on to the header and footer settings. For your normal style (when writing a fiction book), you will need to select 'header on' and 'footer on', but if you plan to have a different heading on the left and right pages for a non-fiction book, untick 'same content left/right'. This means if you want to have different headings on the top of your pages you can. In this book, 'Rachael Hardcastle' is on the left and 'Preparation' is on the right. You can tick this button on the 'footer' part because the only thing we'll be putting in the footer will be page numbers, and we definitely want them on both sides!

For your plain style pages, do not select to apply a header or a footer at all because they aren't needed. These blank pages should be used on the left-hand-side only; preferably, we want all our new chapters to start on the right hand-side.

- Header on
- Footer on
- Untick 'same content left/right' so you can have your author name on one side and the title on the other

Applying Page Styles

When it's time to begin a new chapter, move your cursor to the end of the final sentence. Go to 'Insert', then choose 'Manual Break' and select the page style you need from the drop-down list.

If your chapter ends on the right-hand-side, you'll need to select a plain/blank style for the next page which will be on the left, then immediately go back to 'Insert', 'Manual Break' again and this time select to insert a normal page style for the next page, which will be on the right. This will ensure the next chapter starts on the right-hand side and includes a header/footer.

Remember, if you're writing a non-fiction book, you would select the page style that matches the next chapter.

Headers and Footers

If you want to add page numbers (aka pagination) within your footers, you can click into the footer (or double click depending on the programme) and then go to 'Insert'. Select the 'Footer' option. Page numbers are important but are sometimes omitted from children's picture books as they would ruin the spread.

To add titles within the headers, you can double click in the boxes and type normally. You can also choose how the text looks (font, size, colour, position, etc.) using the options in your toolbar.

Usually, the title of the book is shown on the left header and the chapter title/section is on the right. You could replace one with the author's name if you're writing fiction. I like to centre the content in my headers and footers. Some writers prefer to sit their page numbers on the outside edges.

Images

If you're paying someone to design/format your interior and cover, this next section probably won't apply to you. It's likely your designer will already have dealt with this part of the publishing process and prepared everything in advance. If you're going it alone, I'm going assume in this section that you have a basic working knowledge of photo editing software

Preparation

such as Photoshop, GIMP or even Canva or Kittl.

An important thing to remember is that when you're inserting images into your manuscript, we need to be sure they are set at 300dpi (dots per inch) or more in a CYMK colour profile. Colour profiles and image quality can be set up and selected in your photo editing software's settings.

When the manuscript is ready, ensure you export it as a 'PDF' or 'PDF for Print' in a 1-up format. This means as you scroll through the document, pages should not be side-by-side—it's one page beneath the other.

If you're inserting images with a white rather than transparent background, be sure to check you have selected to print on white paper and *not* cream. Some platforms will limit your options anyway. If you don't, your images may be surrounded by an ugly white box.

Online platforms like Canva and Kittl and software such as GIMP are a great place to start. Canva and Kittl are free to use with the option to upgrade for access to some extra tools and benefits. GIMP is also free but needs to be downloaded to your computer.

You can visit canva.com, kittl.com and gimp.org for more information.

Further in this section, I'll explain how to insert your images to ensure they are accepted by the printer, and how to factor in the bleed.

Contents Page

To insert a contents page, first ensure you have correctly labelled your headers. Highlight the heading or chapter title, and then at the top of the page you will see a drop down or perhaps boxes that give you heading options to select. Normal text may be 'text body'. Use heading 1 for titles, and headings 2 and 3 for sub-headings. By all means change the design of these if the standard ones aren't pretty enough.

Once you have these formatted, you can click 'insert' and then go to 'Indexes and Tables'.

You can give the list a title, for example 'Table of Contents', then choose the way you want it to look.

If you're writing a novel, you don't need to include a contents page or an index.

Bleed

So, what on *earth* does 'bleed' mean? It may sound over-complicated but basically, it's a printing term used to describe content which extends beyond where the book is trimmed—applying mostly when you have images or content that covers the entire page like in a children's picture book. This book, as an example, does not have bleed because there is nothing but white space at the edges.

Imagine that you are sliding your book beneath a guillotine—picture the blades coming down on the outside edges to ensure it has a nice, straight finish. CHOP! You have to keep anything important well

Preparation

within those boundaries to prevent it from being cut off. So bleed is usually 0.125" at the outside edges, top and bottom of the page.

For books with a coloured interior, some platforms like Ingramspark require a blank space in the margin (aka the 'gutter'), also of 0.125" which looks like a white strip so their system can distinguish between what is the content and what is the paper.

They do not require the inner margin to accommodate that extra 0.125" though, so you'd set that up as normal—you just need to make sure your image stops short of the spine by that distance.

Your calculation for bleed would need to be the size of the page (5x8" for example), plus the bleed your printer requires on three sides (0.125" top, bottom and outer). Then your images should cover the full page but stop 0.125" from the spine on the inside).

If you have a full-page spread in image form like in a children's picture book, you would have to cut that long full-spread image in half and put each half on the left and right page, with a white gutter as above in the middle. It would, to the naked eye, look absolutely fine when you open the book, but in the spine of the book there would be a slight gap.

A 'spread' is a term used for a pair of facing pages when you open a book—two pages that sit opposite one another and trim is just the term sometimes used for the size of the book (aka the dimensions).

Be sure to check your last page is blank and that your page count is divisible by two. Simply add an additional blank page if necessary.

Additional Technical Terms

These can be fixed and adjusted in your paragraph settings, and all you need to do is highlight the paragraph you want to amend and right-click, then select 'Paragraph' to access the options.

- Alignment: When you see straight text at both sides of a page (like in this book) it's called 'justification'. Straight text on one side but untidy on the other is called 'ragged'.
- When choosing where to start a new chapter, consider the right-hand side of the page. This is called 'recto'. You may notice this is sometimes opposite a completely blank page on the left which is called 'verso'. Both together make a spread.
- Widows and orphans unbalance your text. A widow is when the last line of a paragraph at the bottom of a page is left at the top of the next page by itself. An orphan, however, is when the first line of a paragraph is left alone at the bottom of a page, and the rest of the text continues to the next. Sometimes, it's easier to just move a paragraph/section to a new page.
- Leading is the space between lines of text.
- Rivers are the spaces between words.
- Kerning is the adjustment of spaces between certain letters.

Preparation

Dialogue

Formatting dialogue for your debut book can be tricky and confusing. My advice depends entirely on what's being said and who by. Here are a few examples and I've put the things you need to make note of in bold and underlined them, followed by an explanation why.

*"Hello, Rachael**,**" **s**aid John**. "H**ow are you today?"*

Dialogue usually ends with a comma before the closing speech marks, followed by a lower case action such as 'said'. If what they are saying can be split into two sentences like in the above example, you can use a full stop, then a capital for the start of the next part of the speech.

*"Hello, Rachael. How are you today**?"** **s**aid John.*

In this second example, we're saying the same thing in a slightly different way. There are still two sentences but they haven't been separated by the writer with action. Although we end with a question mark and not a comma, we still use a lower case 's' in 'said' because this action relates to the speech it just followed.

*"Rachael**,"** **s**aid John**, "h**ow are you today?"*
*"Rachael**,"** **J**ohn said**, "h**ow are you today?"*

These examples show John is using one single sentence, but the writer has chosen to split it in half with action. Because this is two halves of the same sentence, we can use commas at either side. Remember, names should always be capitalised no matter their placement.

"Rachael!__"__ J__ohn wasn't sure she'd heard him__,__ "__H__ey, Rachael!"

The writer, in this next example, has chosen to separate the two sentences with an extended explanation of John's actions. As this is separate to the speech itself, we treat this as we would any other new sentence and punctuate accordingly. However, in the example below, you can see the explanation leads into the second sentence of dialogue, so we use a comma to show this.

"Rachael!__"__ J__ohn wasn't sure she'd heard him so he said__,__ "__H__ey, over here, Rachael!"

If the speaker is then quoting someone else, we would use double speech marks "like this" for the dialogue itself and single quotation marks 'like this' for the quotation within it.

"__I met John the other day and he said, '__I'm running so late!__'__ and I told him to hurry,__"__ Emma said.

It doesn't matter which way around you use these, as long as you stick with your choice throughout the manuscript.

Convenience

Before you choose your book's dimensions, consider if the overall size and weight will be more of an inconvenience to your reader than appealing. Sure, larger books suggest more value for money and, potentially, a full series or collection if they love the characters. Until they pick up the book and read the first part, how will they know if they want the full series?

If the book is heavy (and/or too thick), are they going to want to read it for any length of time if it causes their arms to ache? Will it be too heavy to take in their hand luggage when they travel? Does the extra weight and bulk mean you'll have to increase the price, or that it will be awkward to transport to and from events?

Some readers love hardbacks with dust jackets because they are pretty and the dust jacket acts as a bookmark. Others find them awkward and instantly remove the cover.

Consider, also, the margins of the book. Set these wide enough to allow for a comfortable thumb position on the outer edges (without covering any of the text) and to prevent readers having to crack the spine to see it.

For an adult book, you should use size 12pt font or above to ensure it's large and easy enough to read. You may sometimes get away with size 11pt. Of course, with children's books, you can be more creative, and large print editions might also be beneficial.

Step Three - Cover Design

Basics

Before you even think about designing your paperback cover, ensure your manuscript is finished and fully formatted. You need to know the final page count, and therefore spine width and thickness, first. Most platforms will offer a generator tool for you to download a template, which you can then export into design software like GIMP.

You have less than one second to grab a reader's attention when they are shopping online. When people say they don't judge a book by its cover, they're lying (even though the cover may not *consciously* be their main concern).

Star ratings and reviews on covers might look impressive, but they also need to be from someone relevant or exciting, rather than just Amazon reviewer comments and friends' star ratings. By all means, please include endorsements and recommendations if you have them, though.

If you're designing your cover yourself, learn the basics of software such as Photoshop or GIMP (a free equivalent). There are tons of free and cheap design tools available, so there is no excuse for a poor cover design. Alternatively, you can purchase pre-made covers which do the job just as well.

Be sure any text on your cover is clear and easy to read even as a thumbnail (a small picture, like on an Amazon product page), but above all, it needs to be suitable for your genre and target audience. Comic Sans is not acceptable—there are lots of free, fun alternatives that look and feel much more professional.

Visit a website such as 1001fonts.com and browse what they have to offer, ensuring the license is free for commercial use and free to download. You can filter out any that are not when you search so you don't break any rules and my advice would be to take a screen capture of where you got that font and save it somewhere just in case.

Larger images are going to dominate the reader's attention on a book cover and will be the focal point, but you're more likely to grab their attention if it's centred on the page, particularly if it's surrounded by white space. I prefer simpler covers with a main feature in the centre.

A reader's eye will be drawn to the larger text first, so if you're writing non-fiction consider what you want them to pay the most attention to.

Also, think about whether the cover will look good and read well in black and white. Some e-readers won't display the images in colour and equally, if you're not using POD, textures and foil on a cover may not replicate on the digital edition, so you'll need to tweak that slightly.

Preparation

Character Covers

If you have a face on the front cover, your reader will naturally follow that person's line of sight, so have them looking at something relevant to set the scene. Characters at the edge of a page should look inwards (because otherwise, they are looking at something the reader cannot see), and remember that characters on your cover don't have to match their description in the book perfectly. Readers have an imagination and will picture your characters differently anyway—let them make up their minds and respect their intelligence.

One of my characters in *The Chronicles of Pandora* is a young blonde with a small frame and a bubbly personality. I imagined her to be petite and excitable. Despite the description of the character being in the book, a friend admitted a few months after its release that she imagined this character as a sporty redhead. This proves my point—readers will imagine them in their own way for their own reasons.

Dust Jackets

Dust jackets are extra slips of paper which cover the hardback book beneath. They have two flaps which tuck inside the book at the front and back. Some authors like to include their photo (sometimes called a head shot) and a short bio on the back cover or on the rear inside flap. It's also quite common to see the price and blurb on the front inside flap instead of the back. Reviews occasionally replace them.

Your ISBN and barcode should be on the back cover, and your publisher's logo (if you have one) at the base of the spine. Some books display the genre and available formats near the ISBN, too.

Duplex

Duplex-enabled titles have text or pretty designs and images printed on the inside cover itself. Occasionally, this is where you will see the reviews. There is often a higher cost for this.

Bevelled Edges

Books that are bevelled have untidy page edges. They can be an aesthetic addition to paperback or hardback editions, and it's a binding technique used to cut the pages into angles. Most POD companies do not offer bevelled edges, but a local printer might.

Series

Books in a series should appear that way; make it clear that those books are by the same author and take place in the same universe. Take a look at your favourite series. You will notice these covers are similar in appearance without being identical.

When listing the book/s with retailers, you can

often complete a 'series' field to provide the name and number of the book. This helps the retailer to group them correctly and guide customers to books two, three and four, or help them buy a whole bundle of them.

Most serialised fiction will include the number of the book of the spine or even on the front cover. You can list the correct reading order on one of the first pages inside the book.

Summary

Most platforms will offer you guidelines when it comes to printing (and they are all different, so if you're using a few, be sure to check each individually). You can download templates if this makes life a little easier.

If you're using a company like Ingramspark, you'll need to ensure you're submitting high-quality PDF documents for both your cover and the interior (300 dpi+) and in a CMYK profile, which stands for cyan, magenta, yellow and black.

The number of pages in your book—and whether you've chosen white or cream pages—will determine the thickness, so you should *always* wait to download any templates until after your interior file is ready. If you have entered the ISBN when creating your template (or the book's price and other information), this can sometimes be generated onto the template itself, and you will need to ensure that information remains in place. Remember, if you change the price at a later date and you have included that on the back, you'll have to then amend the cover too.

Though full-colour books can be more attractive, particularly if it's for children, black and white is also an option and can reduce the cost. If you're choosing to print in black and white only (excluding the cover) then you'll need to check it looks good by ordering a proof copy before you publish. Upload the e-book version to your e-reader for the same purpose.

Different e-readers work in different ways because they have various features and display options, so you should check those black and white images are still attractive and easy to see both on and off-screen. Try downloading Kindle Create, which lets you view what your book on each type of device will look like.

If you upload your book to your chosen platform and it gets rejected, go through their specifications one at a time to ensure you have met their requirements:

- Did you export the document to the correct size?
- Did you use the correct colour profile?
- Are your images the correct resolution?
- Did you cover the template provided, or have you left space/s?
- Is it the correct format (PDF)?
- Have you embedded your fonts (this is often done when you are exporting the document)?

Step Four - Pricing

Basics

If you price your book too high—higher than the bestseller in your genre, for example—readers may not be willing to invest in an unknown author. Price too low, however, and they could be suspicious the book isn't worth more. Before you attend a signing or list a book online, remember to do your research. Ask yourself:
- What are books of the same thickness and dimensions selling for in your genre?
- What's the most you could charge and the least you could charge?
- Are you making a profit given the book's printing and shipping (production) costs?

Ask a selection of people from your target audience if after seeing the book in person, would they be prepared to pay the prices you've come up with? Physically holding the book and flicking through it will allow them to judge its worth. Don't expect an accurate response based on photographs or digital mock-ups alone.

Be sure the e-book is cheaper than the paperback,

and the paperback is cheaper than the hardback. Some authors only discount by £1 between each, others by more and some by 50%.

USP

Now it's time to think about what makes your book so special. This is what we call a 'unique selling point' and we have to ask ourselves:

- What makes it stand out from the others in the same genre?
- Why should readers buy from *you* and not from other authors in your category?
- When you're at an event, why will customers approach you and not the author sitting next to you; how are you going to stand out and get their attention?

Your answers to these will create your unique selling point (USP). Imagine you're in an elevator with a famous author and they ask, 'so, what's your book about?' You need to have an interesting answer prepared; something you can say before the elevator comes to a halt and you lose them. Your pitch needs to make them want to ride an extra two floors just so they can hear more, so it should be clear and concise.

When I'm at an event, I put in extra effort too; even at a craft fair where you are the only author in the room, people need to be drawn to your table. Why should they buy your books for a Christmas gift and not a candle?

Preparation

Decorate your display so you stand out in the crowd, and elevate a little if you can using book stands.

Having your books flat on a table may look a bit boring, and passers-by won't be able to see you in a crowded room; those who don't want to approach immediately need to be able to see and read what you're about, so having a tiered book stand (or two symmetrical ones) will help.

You can also try a roller banner with a QR code to make learning more about you easier. You may not sell a book there and then, but they may go home and download an e-book later.

Every fish in the publishing pond has a unique scale that allows them to shine.

QR Codes

A QR code is a two-dimensional code (often seen as a black and white square-shaped pattern) that can be scanned by a device. This identifies a link, which takes you to more information. For example, a reader scans your QR code on a poster and is taken to your website's link, where your author bio and blog can be found.

There are websites where QR codes can be generated for free. Some design tools will also allow you to generate these codes.

Sale or Return

You should ask a book store in advance of your event if they are willing to take stock for their shelves if a book signing is a success. Let them know this can be on a sale-or-return basis, and the stock can be signed.

If you don't know what 'sale or return' means, it's exactly as it says on the label. If the books don't sell, the store can return them to you. This means they may not pay you in advance for those copies as a refund will be due if they need to send them back, so don't be disappointed if this happens. It's fairly standard and, to be honest, makes perfect business sense. The shop gets some free stock for their shelves and if the book sells, you make money (and so do they). If not, they can give them back and it's no harm done. It just means you may be down a few books until either happens.

Some chain book stores have stickers or labels that say 'signed by the author' so customers know in advance they're getting a special edition. If you can get some of those (or even provide them) this would be handy. The same goes for having the price on the back of the book. Some authors like to keep the price off the back cover during the printing process so it can be changed easily. I would recommend this. You can always price with stickers later, and some stores will want to do this themselves anyway.

Clarify exactly what percentage of the royalties the store expects (most will take 30-40%), and be sure you're still in profit afterwards.

Preparation

Royalties

Here's a simple calculation* to figure out how much you're making from each sale at a store signing, based on an example where your book costs the customer £6.99 at the checkout (yours may be more or less, so this is just to show you how it all works). Imagine the store are taking 40% of the royalties.

Divide £6.99 by 100 to calculate what 1% of your price is.

6.99 / 100 = 0.0699

Times the answer by the book store's percentage (40%). You may need to round this up/down.

0.0699 x 40 = 2.796 aka £2.80.

Do the same for the remaining percentage (60%), which on the day is your cut.

0.699 x 60= 4.194 aka £4.19.

Adding both these together should equal £6.99, the original price you set for the book. Then you know your calculations are correct. You may need to round up/down again as you did before.

*In short, your calculation is: **cost of your book / 100 x royalty percentage.**

Now, using your publisher's or printer's online system, figure out how much you are paying to order your stock. Most companies will offer cheaper rates for ordering in bulk (even if only by a few pence), so my advice would be to work this out based on 20, 50, 100 or more copies. Some may even tell you how many fit in a box, so you could choose to order that way. Remember to include any handling fees and delivery charges in your total, then divide that by however many books you're going to order to calculate the cost per book.

If the company offers slower printing and shipping rates to keep costs lower, providing you don't need them urgently, go with the basics. This means your profit per book will be higher, but try and opt for an option where delivery is insured and can be tracked.

As an example, for 100 books including postage and handling fees, an order might cost you £310.00. Again, we are using this as a random example.

For this calculation, that works out at £3.10 per book.

310 / 100 = 3.10.

You should be making more per book in your 60% than it costs you to have that book printed and shipped to your home address. You need to break even at the very least to make selling and stocking a book with that store worth your time. To figure this out, simply minus the cost per book from the 60% figure you calculated earlier.

Preparation

4.19 (your 60%) - 3.10 (cost of production) = 1.09.

That £1.09 is your profit per book. If what you're making in that 60% is *less* than what it costs to produce the book (for example you're paying £3.10 per book but only making £2.80), it wouldn't be worth your time selling with that particular store because you're losing money. That doesn't mean to say you shouldn't stock a small number with them for publicity purposes if that book store is well known, but you should know in advance what you'll earn.

When I release a new book, I *always* calculate what I'll make based on 30%, 35%, 40% and 45%. Then, when I'm planning a signing and that store tells me what they'll be taking, I already know if it's a good idea and how many I can order in a batch. It may be a good idea to create a little chart in your notebook.

Charitable Donations

You should also factor in any donations to charity. If £1.09 is your profit per book (as above) and the charity whose logo you're using on the cover is expecting to receive 50p per sale, your profit is now only 59p.

1.09 – 0.50 = 0.59.

The use of a logo may increase interest and sales, which is a good thing, but if donating to them means you're making a loss per book, an increase in sales will only cost you money instead. Of course, if you're giving away all your profits to the charity knowingly, then you can ignore what I've just said.

Remember industry costs can change, too. If your printer's prices increase, so will yours. This means you will be paying more per book and you may need to increase your prices to ensure you remain in profit. For this reason, it's a good idea to check and re-calculate regularly (and why it's also a good idea *not* to print the price on the back and use stickers instead). You would have to upload a new cover with the new price on (and pay any upload fees) if this happens.

I've fallen victim to this before when I switched to a different platform, so it's something to keep in mind.

Expenses

If you're at an event where you've paid in advance for your stall/table, that event shouldn't really expect to receive royalties for any books you sell that day. This means your profit per book will be higher, but you will need to factor in how much that table has already cost.

As an example, you may sell £150.00 worth of books, and may only have paid £100.00 for them in the first place, meaning you're £50.00 in profit. If you paid £30.00 to hire the table that day, your profit is actually only £20.00. Also factor in the following:

- Fuel. Did you have to drive a long way?
- Food. Have you eaten lunch?
- Accommodation. Have you had to stay overnight in a hotel?

Preparation

- Signage. How much did the banner cost you to make?
- Promotional materials. How much were your bookmarks and leaflets, your business cards and giveaways?

Keep all this in mind when you plan your event and set your prices. If you can have some smaller, cheaper items on sale also (maybe some bookish pins, bookmarks, pens or keyrings), you can boost your earnings that way.

Retailer Discounts & Returns

Some publishing platforms like Ingramspark will allow you to set a retailer's discount and choose whether to allow returns. Chain book stores will prefer to order books they can return if they are unable to sell them, but I generally select *no* when it comes to returns so I do not risk surprise charges.

With regards to the retailer's discount, some will suggest you set this at 55% because it will make the book more attractive to chain stores. I disagree.

I covered this earlier in the book in brief, but here are a few reasons why I would recommend setting a lower percentage initially.

I would never accept lower royalties just because I want to hold off for a chain book store to order my work. The truth is, they may *never* order it and unless I visit each of their stores individually to check the shelves, there's no way to find out if they ever did. In the meantime, I may have had 100 orders from Amazon and earned less for those sales because of it. If I had lowered that percentage to 40% sooner, the royalties for those 100 sales would be higher (and book stores can still order copies if they wish).

The discount you set should also be tailored to your book's needs. By this, I mean if you're expecting to sell more e-books through an online retailer like Amazon than in brick-and-mortar stores like Barnes & Noble, your book will still be attractive to those online retailers at 40%, and some may even be able to offer a discount and still make money. Never assume that because you haven't chosen 55% that nobody will list or stock the book. Some independent stores may struggle to offer their customers a discount and to make anything worth their effort if you select less, but it really depends on what your goals are, and what you want from the book you've published.

Keep in mind that most independent books won't sell more than around 250 copies in a lifetime (for that book). Yours might sell more so this is by no means a way to put you off. Surely for those sales, you would like to receive as many of the royalties as you can, so you can use that money to fund another book?

ATTENDING EVENTS

Organise An Event

Perhaps you're looking to set up an event yourself, or at least initiate an event by contacting a local library, school or bookshop. There are a few things you should include in an initial email or letter to the host/s.

Firstly, use a professional layout; write any e-mails as you would write a letter. Be sure to address it to the correct person in the correct department, and spell their name right. If the person's name can be used for both a male or female, check which it is so you can correctly refer to them.

Set up your e-mail signature if you haven't already done so because it will save time at the end. Your email signature is the information you put on the footer, where your name and contact information is. It should be clear and easy to read in a standard font (avoid Comic Sans or anything too handwritten-looking). In Outlook, you can do this through your account settings.

Then think about why they should help you. Before you write to anyone, make a list of the benefits to that company/store. Then make a list of the benefits to you. Their benefits should outweigh yours; they need an incentive to host this event with you and must get something from the experience, whether this is an increase in traffic or financial compensation in the form of sales or otherwise. However, be sure to include how it will benefit you, too. If you're local, they may be happy to support you because of those reasons. They should know how.

Consider, can you donate a free book to the location? If they can see the quality of your work beforehand and meet you in person, will they be more likely to agree to host an event?

Your e-mail should be positive and inviting and should be thoroughly spell-checked and proofread. If you are sending the same one to several people, be sure you have changed any reference to a name/company each time, that the pronouns are correct, and that all your links work. There's nothing worse than receiving an e-mail that isn't addressed to you.

Here is an example of a standard e-mail. I have used a similar template in the past and received a positive response, but you can amend it as necessary.

FAO [Manager Name]:

Good Morning/Afternoon,

I'd like to query how I can arrange a book signing with your store, please.

At the moment, I'm working with [names of other stores] to promote my existing books, [names of books]. However, on [date], I'll be releasing a brand new [genre] book called [name of book], which I'm

Attending Events

really excited about.

I have a lot of promotional ideas for my events this year, which will include [plans so far]. For this reason, I'm expecting to have a few busy days. This book is important to me because [reasons/ benefits to you and the store or your community]. If you'd be interested in working with me for the launch, I'd love to arrange a book signing at your store for [date] for a [full or half-day] visit.

[Name of the store] has also just taken some of my existing books to stock on their shelves; if you're pleased with the number of sales of [name of new book] at the end of the day, I'd be thrilled to leave a few extra signed copies with you, too on a sale-or-return basis.

Please feel welcome to contact me at any time via [telephone number and email address] to discuss, and thank you for your time and consideration.

I look forward to hearing from you soon.

Kind Regards,

[Signature]

'FAO' should be in bold, and you should try to learn the person's name rather than simply stating 'FAO Manager'. You can also replace 'your store' on the first line to the name of the shop itself. These are things you will have to double-check before you copy and paste it to anyone else—they personalise the query.

'This book is important to me because' is your prompt to explain why you wrote the book, and why you're promoting it in this way. If you wrote a book about recycling, this would be your opportunity to explain why recycling is important to you and how they can get involved—how will hosting a signing with this store help to spread the word?

Larger stores can be very busy during the working week and some offices will be closed on a weekend. You'll need to be patient; a reply may not appear in your inbox that same day but that's OK—they're not ignoring you.

Usually, I allow 1-2 weeks (5-10 working days) before I send a polite follow-up email, just to check they did actually receive it. It might have gone into their 'junk' folder because you haven't previously emailed them. I've had instances in the past where an e-mail was opened by someone who then went on holiday before they had time to respond, so it wasn't seen by other members of staff (or they assumed it was already being dealt with). I've also addressed e-mails to regular contacts who were no longer working at that company (unbeknownst to me), so their e-mails were lost in the system. It took a polite follow-up e-mail or phone call to the store to learn who'd replaced them and update my contacts.

I keep chasers brief and polite. I also offer to call in (if the store is local) at a time suited to them or give them a call as/when they have availability.

If I still don't receive a reply within another 2 weeks, *then* I assume they are not interested and I move on. Sometimes they'll reply later and take me by surprise. Sometimes, they never respond at all. The trick is not to take their lack of response personally;

Attending Events

they will field hundreds of e-mails each week, many of them asking for similar things and, unfortunately, they just can't say yes to everyone.

If they do say yes, be sure to thank them. As the date of the event approaches (7 days beforehand), send an e-mail or give them a call to check they are still happy for it to go ahead. This is important because although they agreed, it may not have been written on their calendar, they may have double-booked, or something last-minute may have cropped up. Of course, they may also have simply forgotten. You don't want to arrive in a room of confused faces and unprepared members of staff. This happened to me once, and it was awkward.

Here is an example of an e-mail you might send for this purpose:

I'd just like to confirm for [date] that you are still happy to host a book signing for [name of book] which was released on [date].

Please see attached a poster advertising the event and if you require any other promotional materials, please do not hesitate to contact me. I will be sure to bring the books, a banner, leaflets and bookmarks on the day.

Thank you again and I look forward to seeing you soon.

When the event is over, send them another e-mail thanking them for their support and let them know how much you enjoyed it, even if you didn't. Remember to always be polite and enthusiastic.

You can attach any invoices to this e-mail, and ask them for copies of any photos they took (and permission to use them), but the money should be the last thing you mention.

Here is a short example:

Thank you to [name of store/person] for hosting my book signing today. I enjoyed the experience and would love to work with you again.

I noticed [name] took a few photos and I'd love to see them. If you're happy to give me permission to use them, I can also tag your store on socials and put them on my website's gallery.

Please see attached an invoice for the books that were sold, as requested.

If you need anything further, please feel welcome to contact me at any time.

If you're including more information about your book or yourself, and are considering putting together a pack for the recipient, here are a few things you might want to consider including.

The event isn't just about you and your books. How can you make this event matter as much to the host as it does to you, and what can *you* do for *them*? Can you help them to raise some funds and attract new customers in some way?

Will a donations pot make any difference? If you're supporting a local library or a charity, can you give a percentage of your profit to the cause and encourage others with spare change to do the same, even if they don't make a purchase? Can you offer your

Attending Events

spare time in exchange for their help? If you are unable to volunteer at the venue, can you attend other events they are hosting to increase the numbers and show your support?

Advertise well in advance (months, not weeks) and send the venue lots of promotional material to make their jobs easier. Let them know how you plan to market the event and, if possible, send along a marketing plan.

Some schools are cashless and when approaching parents, they might use a system rather than physical letters. Parents will get a notification or a 'ping' with updates. In this case, they will likely prefer digital copies of promotional materials to avoid having to print everything out.

Here is an example of what your proposal might include:

- A professional header with your contact information and logo.
- The date and time of the proposed event and how long you require their venue for.
- How much will the event cost to host (hopefully nothing) and how much will you charge for entry? Who benefits from these charges?
- What *is* the event? What will happen and why? Is there a schedule?
- Why have you chosen their venue?
- Benefits to the venue/host and benefits to the

author.
- How do you plan to promote it?
- Will local media be involved? Is the venue expected to notify the media?
- Are there any special guests attending?
- Thank them and remind them of your contact details and availability.

Sign and hand-deliver this if possible. If not, post or e-mail it. Follow up with a phone call or an e-mail if you don't hear back within 10 working days.

Setting Up E-mail Signatures

An e-mail signature is a pre-written chunk of text automatically added to a new or reply e-mail. You can add/remove information from the recommended content below based on what's relevant to you and your company. If you don't want this to show on all your e-mails (such as to friends and family), be sure to set up a variety of signatures to use at your leisure.

- Your name
- Your role
- The company name
- Your contact information including a telephone number, email address, and PO Box.
- A link to your website or socials
- Your office hours

I like to use a splash of colour in my signature to separate it from the rest of the e-mail, or symbols for the contact information. My name and my company name are usually in pink because it's one of my favourite colours. Alternatively, you can use bold.

What Happens At Events...

When it comes to signings and festivals, you'll never really be able to predict your success or estimate how many books you'll sell before you arrive. There are too many uncontrollable factors, though this doesn't mean we shouldn't be prepared and enthusiastic.

Success is more likely with research and preparation—get plenty of stock, advertise well in advance and, of course, keep your branding clear and consistent. This means if you have a logo, make it visible and if you have a mission statement, make that visible, too (and discuss it openly).

Generating some social media excitement beforehand can't hurt either, but while your product may be top-notch, sales will still rely on how busy the event and/or location is in general; you can't sell ten books to zero visitors, neither can you sell a product to women if only men attend.

Get To Know Your Customers

Understanding your target audience is important so we can figure out exactly who we're selling to. Think about who you wrote the book/s for and what your ideal reader looks like.

Demographics
- Where do they live?
- Are you their local author?
- Do they live where the book is set?

Age
- How old are they?
- Is your book too old or too young for their reading level?
- Do they have children?
- Can your book be read together as a family—can it be passed down to a younger sibling when the customer grows?
- Is it perfect for bed time or for a school bag?

Needs and preferences
- Are they shopping for a book to solve a specific need?
- Are you writing a non-fiction or self-help book, maybe in a particular niche?
- What genre do they read?
- Are you writing in a unique or niche genre?
- Do they prefer paperbacks, hardbacks, e-books or audiobooks?
- Are you trying to sell e-books to people without e-readers?
- What formats do you have available?

Just being present at an event is not enough to sell the

Attending Events

book no matter how beautiful and interesting it is, or how pleasant you are. Don't get me wrong, though, you *must* learn how to speak to people in a friendly, yet professional manner. Because people don't like to be sold to. I have crossed the street to avoid a salesperson with a clipboard before. It's annoying and time-consuming, especially when you're heading to your favourite store or are late for your bus.

Approach people with a greeting to gain their attention, but accept some may not return it (or may even go out of their way to avoid and ignore you, maybe even insult you!). Brush any snarly or rude remarks off, then carry on without allowing your smile to waiver or your passion to fizzle. You could simply try 'good morning' and a smile.

Remember that you cannot please everyone, nor should you try. If we all enjoyed the same things, the world would be a very boring place. Choose your battles carefully.

Once you've gained someone's attention and are engaged in polite conversation, ask if they're a reader and if so, their genre preferences. Usually when you ask someone how they are, they reply positively and then, to be polite, ask how you're doing. This is an ideal opening to widen the conversation.

> "Good Morning!"
> *(Hesitant, maybe in passing)* "Good morning."
> "How are you today?"
> *(Stops to respond)* "I'm good thanks, are you?"
> "I'm great! May I ask if you're a reader?"
> *(Hesitantly replies)* "Uhm, yes I am occasionally."

"Is there anything specific you like to read?"
(Smiles and looks at your books) "Mostly crime."

This chat will establish if they are shopping for themselves or somebody else. If you get a good feeling from the conversation, you could even ask their name. A person's name is their favourite word and referring to them by the name they provide will show respect. For example, if they tell you their name is Rebecca, avoid calling them 'Becky'. Using their name shows you have great conversational and listening skills.

Get a copy in their hands by offering it to them in a casual way, but continue to speak while doing so because it's harder for them to interrupt you or refuse to take it. Some might politely put it down, which is fine. If this makes you uncomfortable, you can always tell them they are welcome to pick anything up to have a look in their own time, and if they have any questions, you're happy to answer them.

Tell them about the storyline or what inspired the theme, leaving the conversation at a natural stopping point; one likely to prompt further questions if you can.

There's still no way to guarantee they won't hand the book back (or refuse to take the book off you in the first place), but if they do take it from you, they'll be a little bit more likely to purchase it. Put yourself in their shoes. Having stopped to speak to someone selling a signed and personalised book in your favourite genre, and willingly taken a copy to flick through from that person (rather than just off an unmanned table), how would giving it back and walking away make you feel?

As the author, you're likely to feel disappointed if

Attending Events

a potential customer walks away at the last minute and that's perfectly normal and acceptable. However, it doesn't mean to say it's a permanent rejection. You can always thank them and (if you're well prepared), hand them an attractive flyer or a free bookmark in exchange for their time. Wish them well, and tell them it was lovely to meet them.

"I'm just browsing today, but thanks."
"That's no problem, it was nice to meet you. Would you like a free bookmark to take away with you?"

Any interest is better than no interest, and by standing at your table they're doing you a favour regardless of whether they buy anything.

If you don't believe me, try this. Next time you're out shopping with a friend, find something mundane to gasp and point at, preferably high above you on the opposite side of the street so it's not immediately obvious what you're doing. Ask your friend to play along. Soon, you'll notice others around you will stop or look back to see what's so interesting—curiosity gets the better of us and we don't want to miss out. By standing at your table for a chat, picking up the book or simply reading your banner from a few meters away, they're already generating potential customers by being present. For that, you should be grateful.

Remember that if you ask a customer to take a photo with you for your website or social media, you will make them feel valued. Ask if it's OK to use the photo because parents may not want their children's faces on your Facebook page. If the customer has heard of you before, they'll want to evidence your meeting for friends and family (who may read the book, too). Agree to all photo opportunities and ask that they tag you on social media by giving them a leaflet or business card including this information. It's better to wait for them to share it and tag you than to risk posting it without their consent.

If you have a selfie square or banner featuring a hashtag, that's even better because it does the work for you. They don't need to remember your details because they are already included in the photo. By sharing and talking about it, they're helping to spread the word.

Appearance

I don't know about you, but when I'm heading to an event, everything we've just talked about seems the least of my worries. I'm usually more concerned with small, pointless things. Except, to me, they don't seem so silly at the time.

- Should you stand at the table? No, because that would that feel too much like you're trying to sell something (even though you are) like you're not an important, bestselling author they should be excited about.
- Should you sit? Maybe make them approach as if you're royalty, or is that too professional and will you miss the opportunity to speak to passers-by?

Attending Events

- Do you take a banner or allow the book store to use theirs? Would this mean they don't know who you are, or would a branded banner feel more like a 'real' book signing? Without a banner, surely people will be forced to speak to you to find out who you are and what you're selling, right? Or will having to speak to you put some people off? With a banner, they may not speak to you at all, though.
- How should you display your books? If you stack lots together in a nice neat pile, will people be afraid to touch them or think you haven't sold any? If you stack a few carelessly, won't people feel they need to hurry before you run out, or will they think you're unprepared and messy?

Let me stop you there. First of all, book signings can be exhausting. I'm exhausted just talking about them. You'll be needing a chair, believe me. Whether you use it all day or not is irrelevant. Ask for a chair. Wear some comfortable shoes and, if you feel like you're missing sales by sitting down, get up and move around a bit, but avoid getting in anyone's way or in anyone's space.

Remember, even *I* avoided the lady with the clipboard. It's not a science, merely trial and error. And sure, most popular bestselling authors sit, but they also have long queues managed by store staff and, if they're famous, security. This doesn't apply to you yet. They don't have tons of books and promotional stuff on their table; all they have is a pen because that's all *they* need.

So do what feels comfortable and natural to *you*. Readers may recognise you and if they do, they'll speak to you anyway. Those who don't are going to decide if they want to meet you whether you're standing or sitting, so try not to over-think this. Speaking from experience, you'll give yourself a headache.

Remember, if a friend or family member offers to help you for the day, accept their company. In a busy store, staff may not be able to watch your things while you take a five-minute toilet break or run to the nearest coffee shop. If the store/location allows it, they may also be able to hand out leaflets or bookmarks to generate some interest on your behalf. Then, you can have the best of both worlds—someone standing and someone sitting. Be sure to thank your volunteer/s and cover their expenses too; it might be a long, tiring day. They may also need insurance!

As far as your banner is concerned, yes, you'll be needing one of those. People who don't want to risk being sold to or perhaps don't have the time to stand and chat may still pause to read your banner and grab a leaflet.

Your banner needs to include your photo, a brief bio and a picture of the book cover at the very least. I'd also recommend including your web address and social media details because you'll find people will want to Google you before they say hello (or use a QR code). You could be famous; why would they want to miss your signing? Without speaking to you, people can determine if you're worth their time in seconds via their device these days.

Attending Events

If the store has a backing banner and insists you use that, use it and don't argue. You could still politely suggest they place your branded banner in the doorway to attract passers-by, though, and ensure *that* banner has a poster attached that says 'here today only'. It needs to be securely fastened or propped up for safety. Alternatively, you can use an A-frame—the wooden type you see outside with chalk menus or messages on. If you're in a shopping centre or a public place, check these are permitted first.

Displays, in general, are tricky. They'll vary depending on the location and the event itself. If you're in a book store, keep the display simple and in a similar style to other displays around you. Have plenty of stock visible (and not too tidy!) so people aren't afraid to pick up a copy and believe others have been looking, too.

Have your business cards on display in a plastic holder, which most stationary stores sell. Have bookmarks and/or leaflets at the ready, too. You may need to change your display if you're not getting much traction; avoid building a barrier between you and the readers with books or display units, because this can feel impersonal and too official.

I tend to use two tiered book stands at either side, with the promotional materials in the middle or in front. Then they can see my face and interact with me and I can reach everything if they need help. I have the banner either behind me or off to the side.

Have your prices in a plastic A4 display stand (those where the paper slides between two plastic panes and stands upright at an angle) if you can. If this doesn't work and you feel knowing the prices before speaking to you puts people off, remove the list and encourage people to chat; this is a great opportunity to share your USP.

Lay your books flat, but have them stacked, or use stands if you've got some. You can build them as you'd see bricks in a wall. This, of course, will depend on how thick your books are because the stack/s shouldn't be too high.

People need to see your face and feel like they can approach and chat without having to peer over a barrier. At the front of your stack, have a display copy people can pick up and thumb through. You could also consider using a small plastic book stand to the side of your stack—it doesn't matter if that copy looks used/worn more than the others, but it should still be in relatively good condition. You can always put a sticker on it that says 'display only'.

If you have a small amount of a second book left to sell, include these in the display, especially if that's all you have left. The selling point for these would be 'get them while they last'. If they've sold well—either at that event or previous events, meaning you're down to your last five or six copies—readers may purchase one of those in addition to the book you're promoting in fear of missing out. Tell them, 'I only have these left today; it's the last of my stock'.

If you have more than one book on offer, remember to include bookmarks or leaflets for your other work when you're signing that customer's purchase. Even if they're not interested, if they enjoy the book they've bought and see the quality is high,

Attending Events

they might recommend you to a friend who *does* enjoy those other genres.

Finally, include a note to say thank you and remind them to leave a review.

When you're at a festival, I'd advise approaching your display a little differently. Build it up and back at an angle as you would see in a shop window. Three-dimensional displays with plenty of colour will attract attention, but be sure to sit everything atop a suitable tablecloth (and from experience, check the table is secure first). There's nothing worse than an old, scratched and/or wobbly table beneath a quality product (especially when everybody else's is sparkly and clean). You can use secured boxes beneath additional cloths to create shelves if you need to (make sure they are *absolutely* safe and unmoving!), but I'd recommend purchasing some single book stands so your products are held upright and look inviting instead.

Try to look your best, too. I'm not suggesting you should spend hundreds of pounds on some new clothes and a haircut, but wear something appropriate, clean and attractive. If you're selling a children's book, don't be afraid to wear some brighter colours with prints (or even a costume). If you're writing a book about business and finance, perhaps opt for something a bit more professional (such as a suit, heels and a blouse). Whatever you're writing, you should be approachable and appear to be that subject's guru.

If you're attending an event as a company, uniforms may also be a good idea, or a branded polo shirt to make your employees easily identifiable. And if you need to (or are asked to) ensure you wear identification.

Stock

For your first (maybe ever) event at an unpopular or lesser-known location, I'd advise taking twenty copies. For larger book store events, double it, or for weekend festivals and conferences, you may even want to double it again.

If you're already established and have a platform, you will be able to judge if you'll need more. It's always better to have too many than not enough. Also, if you can discount a little, feel free to do so—current fans or interested readers may not want to miss saving some cash, so they'll be more likely to buy from you rather than ordering online (meaning higher royalties if your calculations are correct). Please be mindful that discounting might eat into your profit, though. Alternatively, you could offer a deal such as 'buy a book and get a keyring half price'.

"It's not all about the money, I just love what I do and want to enjoy the experience!" I hear you say, and you're right. **You should enjoy every minute of every book signing, because you've put your heart and soul into this book and you deserve to soak in the success.** I, too, do this job because I'm passionate about writing and independent publishing, and I want to help as many authors as I can. But, *surely* it would be nice to pay a bill with the profits from your creative career?

As I said at the beginning of this chapter, you're

never going to be able to predict your success on a day-to-day basis; some of those books may return home with you, and that's OK too.

Author Copies

I've often seen authors on social media asking whether they are allowed to sell on the stock they have ordered from their publishing platform. To confirm, once you have paid for and received any 'author copies', these are yours to do with as you please. Some copies show 'not for resale', so I wouldn't advise selling these (though you could give them to friends and family or keep them to look back on). When you order a box of fifty for an event, however, you can absolutely sell these on—that's the whole point of ordering them.

Second-hand Copies

Some authors get upset when they see their books being sold second-hand online. I see this as a compliment; that person thought it good enough to pass on. Lots of readers don't keep books or re-read them, so it makes sense for them to give them away or sell them. It's not personal.

Once they own your book, it's up to them what they do with it. It's the same as buying a book in Waterstones and then lending it to a friend to enjoy on your recommendation.

There's also the brutal reality that they simply may not have enjoyed it. You can't please everyone, so don't feel offended. At the end of the day, they still bought it and you still earned royalties.

Uncontrollable Stuff

How well the book sells could rely on an array of external factors. Like the weather. If it's a bright, sunny day, will people be at the park instead? If it's raining heavily, are people staying at home? Alternatively, will it drive them inside to their nearest store? Check the weather beforehand and plan any important events during seasons where the weather works to your advantage.

If your store has a coffee shop, this can potentially increase sales for you too because people love to buy a book, then sit with a brew and flick through it.

Are you signing books on the same day as a local festival? Could people be attending that instead? Alternatively, if it's near-by will you naturally have extra customers because of the increased traffic?

Is it a holiday or a special occasion? Are you selling more today than you will next month because it's Father's Day? Are you selling more children's books because schools are currently closed for the summer? Is your book about Christmas and you're selling it in December?

Is your book set in (or gives information about) the city you're signing in? Will books about New York sell better in New York? If you're an author from London signing a book in London, will the 'local author' label work for you?

And was the store prepared for your arrival; have

they made the effort to assist and promote you? Was their website updated with details of your signing? Have they offered you an ideal place within their store to sign books, put up posters or used a banner of their own? Did they share the event on social media? Did they seem excited to have you there, greet you nicely and shake your hand? It's easy to judge how invested a store is in the event and how well they think your books will do by the way they interact with you.

These points are by no means an excuse for selling fewer copies at an event, but they are factors you need to keep in mind. A chain store may not roll out a red carpet for an unknown independent author's first event—they don't know you and are (like you) unsure how well the book will sell. Be grateful they've welcomed and accepted you and, as I like to say, just go with the flow and make the best of every moment.

Failure

After a full day's work, perhaps you only sold three copies and the store refused to accept any for their shelves. You're feeling disappointed and you're asking:

- Did I fail?
- Did I let myself and the book down?
- Did I make a fool of myself?

You are not a failure. You haven't let anyone down. You certainly did not make a fool of yourself. **You tried and you were brave.**

Have you heard the saying, 'there's no such thing as bad publicity'? In these circumstances, there isn't. You still sold three copies, and (I hope) took lots of photographs of the display and of you standing proudly outside the store for your website and social media. You need to be associated with their brand because it looks good to potential customers. You gave it your all and you still shook hands with a manager that you may now consider a future contact.

Those images are all over your platform and that's three more people in the world in ownership of something *you* created than there was yesterday.

Some authors make book signings look easy, and they'll brag about how many were sold and how much of a success the entire day was, and you might see their Facebook updates and growl with jealousy because they're making a living from it when you're not. Don't let their confidence consume you.

The truth is, these authors may not have done as well as they say they did and without seeing an invoice or written evidence, you'll never know for sure if it's all for the sake of publicity; if it's a lie to make them look and feel better, clearly it's working because they have sufficiently wound you up. Does 'fake it until you make it' come to mind?

Don't let passion blind you to this industry's uncomfortable reality; it's not a huge money-making business, yet it's still bloody hard work. That hard work deserves a reward and earning money from what you're doing means you can continue to do it in the future. Without it, how are you going to order your next batch of books or your next box of bookmarks?

Attending Events

One of my first 'big breaks' as the owner of my own independent publishing company was with a popular store in the UK. I'd psyched myself up for weeks after receiving news that the manager was willing to host a signing for the paperbacks I had available at that time (and there were several). I enlisted the help of a volunteer, spent some cash on promoting and marketing materials, and we drove my stock several hours away from where I lived to set up, only to find that due to an admin error, we'd been double-booked with another author who was already doing *really* well.

In the few minutes we were waiting to speak with the manager, at least three of their books sold and the customers all went away with photographs and huge smiles on their faces. This author was a superstar, and I... well, *I* was not.

As we were early and not due to sign until the afternoon, we relaxed knowing by the time we'd eaten lunch, our events would no longer clash and we could part ways. However, we soon learned the other author had decided to extend their signing, which would, therefore, overrun into our slot and force us to re-locate to a less visible area of the store. For the first two hours, we had to watch potential customers walk straight to the main table and hand their money and support to someone else, without even noticing us.

Initially, my thoughts were not of anger or of upset, but merely of disappointment. It wasn't fair. In my mind, I knew this was supposed to be my big break and I was an embarrassment to myself and my volunteer. It was supposed to be an event to shine a spotlight solely upon my hard work and dedication to my craft—to my passion and talent. I know now that it's a rather selfish and immature thought, but I'd been really excited and lost a lot of sleep over the preparations, so that's just how I felt. I embraced it.

Internally, I was a panicking train wreck. Externally, I screwed on my most confident smile and got stuck in regardless because, when the other author decided to pack up and leave, I wanted to be ready (and to do my best not to cry).

Eventually, they did leave and the manager moved us. For the hours I spent in that seat, we sold more books than I imagined we would, took plenty of photographs and met some amazing people, including that author (who turned out to be a nice person).

At a signing, try and aim to sell at least four books an hour, which is one book every 15 minutes. That's impressive for an independent author—if you're there between 10am and 4pm (six hours), that's 24 copies!

WORKING WITH OTHERS

External Support

Sometimes, it's handy to gain external support from other companies. If you're writing a book about a particular illness and a local charity has offered to allow you the use of their logo for the cover, there are a few important details you need to work out first.

With some charities, you will need to do plenty of research to ensure your book falls in line with their requirements before you publish. A good example of this would be writing for people with Dyslexia—your book should meet certain requirements and parameters before you advertise it as 'Dyslexia friendly'.

Rather than include the logo on the cover itself, it might be wiser to ask for stickers. Then, if at any time they decide not to support you, their logo can easily be removed from any books you haven't yet sold. This will save you having to spend money on a new batch.

Be sure to find out if the company are expecting royalties from sales that are *not* sold in one of their stores. Does having their logo tie you to them in some other way? Do they expect to receive donations per book sold no matter where you sell the book, such as on Amazon? Can you put a written agreement in place?

Either way, clarify how much they are expecting to receive and if you can afford to do this and still make a profit. Sure, their logo may attract more customers and gain more sales, but if you are now making a loss per book, do you wish to continue?

Don't Rely On Others

This is where I sound miserable. I once received some great advice (on a personal level rather than a business level) which I think transfers well to the publishing world.

'If you don't expect anything from anyone, you will never feel disappointed or let down.'

This may sound untrusting. But, when it comes to waiting anxiously for reviews or BETA feedback, remembering this line can quickly ground you to reality; those roles are voluntary and **you aren't owed anything**.

If they respond late or not at all, there's nothing you can do to fix that. Any reviews or quick responses you do get will be a bonus.

The same goes for book sales. When you publish your book, if you expect to be a multi-millionaire and a famous bestseller, you are likely to be disappointed. However, if you estimate you will sell 100 copies (to family and friends initially) you may then be pleasantly surprised.

Cancellations

When it comes to dealing with other authors or clients (particularly when you're meeting face-to-face), *always* send a message or an e-mail a few hours beforehand to check they can still make it.

I've unfortunately fallen victim to last-minute cancellations and no-shows. As a professional, this can be frustrating, especially if you had to turn others away who needed an appointment. *You* may use a diary, but they may not work the same way.

If after two or three attempted meetings you still have no success—they keep cancelling, they never turn up or they are always *ridiculously* late—it may be time to move on. If you're trying to help for free in your own time, consider it their loss and focus your energy and attention elsewhere. However, if the meeting will result in you getting paid for a service of some kind, then it's up to *you* to make that all-important business decision.

- Do I value my self-respect and time over how much this meeting will pay?
- Is this person taking advantage of me or wasting my time?
- Is it worth the stress and anxiety?

Set a good example. Reply to your emails quickly and efficiently, and treat others in the industry the way you hope to be treated. Keep a diary and attend meetings when you say you will. Let people down *only* when you have no other choice (family emergencies can't be avoided, but you can certainly apologise sincerely).

I'd dread to think there's an author out there disappointed in me because of something I said I'd do but haven't done. It's about keeping your promises (or not making any in the first place unless you're 100% sure you can keep them).

MARKETING

Step One - Websites

Websites act as the hub for your activity as an author. If people want to see the books you have available, upcoming, or find out where they can meet you, they'll Google you and look for a website link. I get so frustrated when I fall in love with a series or an author only to discover they don't have a website for me to look at.

Your social media platforms should all point to your website and your website should link easily to your social media platforms, whilst also acting as a gallery and a blog/journal where readers can keep up to date with what's going on.

If you can, make your website accessible so it can be easily read from a mobile phone or a tablet. Most design platforms like wix.com will offer tools to help you achieve this.

SEO and Keywords

SEO stands for 'Search Engine Optimisation'. Most platforms for web design have the facility for you to make the best of SEO by allowing you to change how (and if) it appears in search engines such as Google. You may be able to change the title of your page/s and include a brief description of them (which should all include keywords). You may also be able to choose keywords for your website itself, so it's easier for potential customers to find.

You must include relevant keywords so when people are searching for your book or your website, they can find you. While you might think 'books about wizards' is a great keyword for your young adult book about a school of wizards, including that as a key phrase is pointless; an already well-known book dominates those results, leaving yours lost somewhere in the mix.

You can check how many results particular keywords return each month with free online tools. Also try publisherrocket.com. But an easier and free tool when you're just starting out would be Amazon's search bar.

Amazon is basically a huge search engine, so in their search bar type in the phrase you might use to find your book. For example, 'young adult books about' and then see what Amazon suggests. You'll see a drop down of potential searches appear beneath. You can consider those popular terms of interest, and choose those most relevant to your book. Note that these can change, though, as trends move on.

Aim to find 15-20 ideal keywords for each of your books and each of these should have a reasonable score if you're using a system like Publisher Rocket. If it's too low then there aren't enough people searching for that keyword, so it would be a bad idea to use it.

However, if your book is in a niche category (something unusual with a specific target audience) then a smaller score may not be such a problem.

If the score is too high then we're back to what I said about the book about wizards—your entry will be completely lost.

Subscriptions

Some authors like to create a subscription service through their website. Readers and fans can receive automatic updates and freebies in exchange for signing up via e-mail to receive correspondence. This doesn't mean the author has the go-ahead to spam them endlessly with offers, news and invitations, though. Just one or two per month to start with, and readers should be able to unsubscribe at any time.

When people subscribe, they can receive a special thank you e-mail with freebies attached. This is in addition to the other e-mails they will receive that month and is a one-off gift—an incentive to join the list.

Pages

Here are some pages you might want to consider adding to your website. Feel free to add more or remove some of them if they aren't right for your book.

- About – your author bio and a photograph of

you (a professional head shot, not a selfie of you in the bathroom mirror. I've seen it before.).
- Gallery
- News
- Events
- Books – details of your available book/s and links to buy them. You could also advertise pre-orders here or make use of a countdown clock to generate excitement.
- Journal/Blog
- Contact – be sure to include your social media links and if you have one, your PO Box address. I would advise against using your home address for obvious reasons.
- Services (if these are offered)
- Testimonials/Reviews
- Pop-ups – on some platforms, you can set up an on-screen pop-up that prompts visitors to subscribe, make a purchase, or review something. Some authors prefer to do this within the first few seconds of visiting a particular page, whereas others like to give people a chance to explore first. These can become annoying and can get in the way, so limit your use of pop-ups and if possible, only display each of them once.
- Landing pages – this is a single, condensed page including the information you'd like your reader to see before anything else. This is often part of your website, but inaccessible from the main home page. It's a link you would give out

to specific people, for a specific reason, such as offering a giveaway, joining a mailing list or buying a discounted book. You could also share information via a video or a short audio clip.

Try to keep your website as up-to-date as possible—my advice is to log in at least once per week to upload new photos, add event dates, etc.

If you're struggling for website ideas and inspiration, research some of the authors you read regularly and see how theirs are laid out and what content they offer. Make a list of five websites you like, and then write a few paragraphs detailing why.

Google yourself and see what the results show. Your website should be one of them—how does it look and what would you change about the listing?

Domains

Consider purchasing your domain (the name of your website such as rachaelhardcastle.com) rather than using free versions offered through platforms such as Wix. As a reader, I would feel far more comfortable visiting an attractive, professionally built website with an easy-to-remember domain than a long, complicated one that's years out of date.

The free domains are fantastic, however, if you're looking to learn how to use that platform's tools or set up a separate blog.

Purchasing a domain is inexpensive and worth every penny. Choose something relevant to you and if your name is common, add 'author' at the end.

Remember that readers need to be able to remember your details and know how to spell them—if they can't find you online for whatever reason, that's one less fan/reader you have.

It's also better to name your website after you as the author rather than your debut book's title. If you produce other books, this may become complicated and the design irrelevant or out of date, particularly if you write across genres. Readers are likely to get fed up of hopping between several websites if you have different domains for different books; it's more convenient to have everything in one place.

Blogs

If you're hoping to learn how to write a blog post from this book then I must apologise. I used to blog often, but soon realised with everything else going on in my life and my workload, I couldn't keep up to posting regularly, which is important if you want to get returning visitors. It works the same as posting content to a YouTube channel if you're giving advice or uploading episodes; always better to have a schedule.

Whilst I can't advise you about blog posts here, I can advise you to make use of that space to post a monthly newsletter or even interview other authors, if this is something that interests you.

When I first started writing, I made a point of posting an author interview every week. I'd scout social media groups for writers and would offer to interview independent authors free of charge in exchange for them sharing it with their fans, readers and followers.

Marketing

This would drive traffic to my website and, hopefully, capture new readers of my fiction at the same time.

I never charged for an interview, but I made it clear to those taking part what it would be used for and how. I used to send an information sheet first and ask authors to sign to state they had fully read and understood. Included were rules such as 'no bad language or sexual references' and that I reserved the right to edit out anything that didn't make sense, fix any spelling issues, and remove the interview at any time.

If you do decide to post an interview, read it thoroughly beforehand and approve the content. Be sure it's not offensive and the questions are suitable. There are several questions you could use to start.

- Why did you become a writer?
- Where do you get your ideas?
- Where do you find inspiration?
- What are your top three marketing tips?
- Who is your favourite author?

Include a link to the author's website/social media in the interview and a photograph or video (something visual) to make it eye-catching. If you can, you should also include keywords, tags and categories to make it easier for future readers to find.

Step Two - Social Media

Like for Like

You may sometimes come across 'like for like' on social media posts. If you 'thumbs up' an author's page, they will do the same for yours in return (or follow, like, share, depending on the platform). Don't get me wrong, I can see exactly why this sort of post is appealing to a lot of new writers; the promise of an increase in page likes in exchange for the click of one button seems easy enough. But, I avoid 'like for like' exchanges for several reasons.

Firstly, they don't offer you genuine readers. The people exchanging these likes are all authors and writers looking to increase their own following. Just because you have a higher number of likes doesn't mean you have their genuine interest (and they won't become customers). They don't last, either. It's easy to hit like on a page and hit unlike one week later. Lots of writers are looking for an increase in likes but will not genuinely like yours in return—a week later (or maybe even a day later) they'll hit unlike quickly and without guilt. When you like a page, you begin to see posts from that page and if you're not interested in the content, you either unfollow or unlike to make it go away. What do you think people who 'liked' your page that aren't interested in you or your books will do when your posts begin to appear on their feed?

They also don't reflect what you believe in. Liking a page without reading anything about the person or their books is a mistake. What if they write about something you find offensive? What if every other sentence they write includes a curse word, or they write erotica which you don't read? What if they're openly rude to other writers in the group, or all they do 24/7 is post 'buy my book'? As an author, you're potentially a public figure and someone who needs to be a positive role model and maintain an image—openly supporting someone that goes against that image (especially if you've done it without realising), can't be good.

I'm sure you're asking how you find people who *will* genuinely like your page, and remain a fan for a long time. There's no magic formula or secret I can give you, but perhaps a few tips. And it starts by being genuine, being honest, being approachable. Overall, be a nice person and post relevant, interesting things to your page. You're a writer, so sharing a Stephen King quote you've seen will interest your followers. Posting a music video with half-naked ladies posing on a flashy car is not relevant, and might offend some of your followers. They're with you for a reason, so give them what they signed up for.

Make use of the page's/platform's features including the 'about' section and ensure you link your website. List events and services and keep them regularly updated. If you change your prices, update

Marketing

the listing. And obviously post photographs of you smiling with your books and at book stores so your readers can see how passionate you are and how much you love your job. This also shows you're active in the business and your community.

When you're releasing a new book, post cover reveals, competitions/polls and live videos if that sort of thing interests you. I don't use ads often, but this is another option. I attend a lot of events where I meet people, handing out leaflets and business cards, bookmarks and other marketing materials, which is where I spend my budget for advertising. However, just because you don't use something like Facebook ads now doesn't mean you can't in the future, so they're something to keep in mind and something lots of authors have had success with.

Post regularly. Keep your readers up to date with what's going on so they remain interested and your posts remain in their feed. Some authors like to stick to a schedule, or schedule posts to go live on future dates.

The more you ask people to buy your book, the less likely they will be to do so. It's annoying and clogs up their feed; they want interesting news items and fun photos to scroll through on their lunch breaks, not to be bombarded by your begging. And it's hard not to talk about yourself or your book, I get it. I'm always tempted to add my website link or mention one of my books when I share something that might help people with their project, but that action in itself draws people to you. Although you didn't write what you're sharing, you're making it easy for them to access something useful. You've just done them a favour.

Paid Advertising

Some platforms will allow you to set up paid advertisements or promotions, which they will circulate to your chosen target audience for a fee. You can narrow the audience down to target specific ages, locations and interests, for example, women aged 30-65+ who read romance in the UK. You can access figures for each ad you set up or each post you 'boost', which means you can see if the promotion is working.

You can also tell these platforms (such as Facebook) what your goal is—do you want people to click a specific link, do you want more page likes? They will automatically calculate how many people you are likely to reach based on how long you run the ad for and what your spending budget is.

Making Friends

In short, my advice is never to accept friend requests from clients, readers, or other authors you have never met in person on social media (on your personal account). Posting and commenting in groups to generate some interest and chatting with them via private message or in the feed is fine, but once you accept a friend request, that person can see things on your profile you may wish to keep private. That's why it's a good idea to have two—one is an account for family, friends and colleagues where I post about holidays, days out, etc. The other is my business page. Here, I post about my books.

Marketing

Because my comments are usually under my personal account because I scroll and see things I'm interested in, I do often get friend requests (and spam/phishing messages from 'professionals' who want to work with me). I have a friendly system to avoid accepting these and use a template response that I amend depending on the person/query. It goes something like this:

Hi, thanks for your friend request! I usually only accept friends and family to my personal account, but I have an author page over at [enter your page link here] where we can talk all things books. If your request was about one of my services, please feel welcome to reply to this message—I'd love to help you further in any way I can. You can also check out my company website [link] and send me an e-mail when you get the chance. Thanks! Please note: I don't respond to any promotional messages, and all scam/phishing messages/emails I receive are immediately reported.

The same advice goes if you're the person sending the friend request. Always ask before you do this either in the comments feed or via a private message, because like me, they may not be comfortable accepting a stranger's invite. If you receive a response like mine, don't be offended. That person has good business and security sense.

Hashtags

Hashtags on social media are words beginning with the symbol # and are used to collect posts and information on a particular topic so those interested in that topic can find and read everything related to it easily. Here are a few of my favourites used across the various platforms of social media:

- #amwriting (sometimes with the genre for example #amwritingfantasy)
- #authorsofinstagram
- #writerslife
- #writerproblems
- #bookstagram
- #ask (followed by author, agent, editor).
- #indieauthor
- #amediting
- Some authors create their own to promote themselves or their books, or to collect posts about their latest release/s.

Social Media Tips

Only plug your book once every ten social media posts. Provide interesting, free content in the other nine, or followers may get fed up with you. If you have an author page, set up an automated response to all private messages, letting readers know it has been safely received and how soon they can expect a reply. Avoid using bad language and

Marketing

sexual references unless this is specific to your genre and target audience. If you work in schools, you may find families searching for you on social media, and it would not be appropriate for them to be met with unsuitable content.

Join and participate regularly in groups on social media, but avoid promoting your website/book via any links unless the rules state you can. If you write non-fiction, commenting and advising others on that specific topic can help readers to see you as a suitable 'guru', which may then lead to book sales or other paid services. But if you're posting links and ads all the time, people will think you're trying to scam them.

Post an 'all about me' or 'all about my book' video to social media—if you have a YouTube channel, this would be a great place to start. Videos can be played in the background, so it's easier and more convenient for readers to learn about you if they don't have time to read a long blog post. Plus, it's visual—colour and personality make selling yourself and your book much more interesting. Share pictures of your book too. Be sure to smile and hold your book up proudly so readers can see it physically exists and looks awesome. They can then make a personal connection between your book and your happy face—they'll want to support someone who looks friendly and proud, and will feel they know you a little better.

Cover reveals can spark excitement. Consider revealing what the book will look like a few weeks before its release. You could run a giveaway or post the first chapter of the book free of charge on your website/blog to generate some interest. Or, set up polls to involve your readers in the creation of the book. If they've contributed, they may be more likely to buy it on release day to see if you listened to their suggestions and feedback.

Some authors like to run their own podcasts or simply appear on other people's to discuss writing and their latest releases. Podcasts are like recorded radio shows that readers can play on-demand and are often serialised. Similarly, you can tour blogs relevant to your genre by completing written interviews for other people; when they post these interviews on their websites, their readers can then follow links to find and purchase your books.

When attending events, make use of live videos if you're comfortable and if it's allowed by the venue, and broadcast what's going on to friends and followers. You can then download those videos and upload them to your YouTube channel, website and blog. It's scary, but consider braving the camera to promote your work through personal videos or 'vlogs'. Remember to smile and be positive—readers should be able to relate to you, make that personal connection and build an element of trust.

When you have some spare time, do a little research and consider signing up for an account with these platforms so you can explore their features, like TikTok. Even if you don't intend to post and promote on them, you can still keep your account private, then follow other authors and learn from their content. Platforms change and some go out of date quickly, which is worth remembering.

Does your Instagram handle match your Facebook

handle, so it's easy for people to identify you across various social media platforms? If not, can you change it so it's easier for them? Have you updated the 'about me' section of your profile, added a professional photo, listed your services or published titles and linked your website?

Summary

It's been said that buyers need to see a product at least seven times before they make a purchase or click a link.

Remember, you're a small fish in a huge pond so marketing a book alone isn't going to be easy. Give yourself a break. You're not going to become a bestselling author overnight. These things take blood, sweat and tears but mostly, they take new ideas and a little time.

Think about how you can get the relevant information to your readers seven times without spamming or irritating them. When one of your marketing techniques doesn't work, don't give up. Log your efforts and the response you got, plus why you feel it went that way. Then move on.

There is absolutely no such thing as 'I've tried everything' and when someone tells me this, my answer is always, 'can you show me a list?'

Decide now what success means to you. Do you want to see your books on the shelves of a popular high street chain store? Do you just want to hold a physical copy in your hands and share it with friends? Do you want to sell 1,000 books in six months? This is always the first question I ask when an aspiring author asks me how to write and publish a book. The advice changes depending on their answer.

Start thinking about what success is and means to you at this early stage because it's much easier to judge how well you're doing if you have standards to measure them against.

You could set five goals and review them quarterly (four times per year). When you achieve a goal, replace it with a new one and, if you can, increase the difficulty level. If you wanted to sell fifty books in six months and easily achieved that, set your next sales goal at 100 books in three months, as an example.

Step Three - Paperwork

Press Releases

A press release gives information on a particular matter and is written as a statement, then issued to the media. There are several sections you need to include in a particular order. In short, these are:

1. Contact information
2. Heading and sub-heading
3. The location and date
4. The text body
5. Any links or calls to action at the end

You can send a press release to local media, book stores and anyone else you feel may want to know about your book's release or related events. Local newspapers and radio stations are a great place to start, and you should attach the press release to an email as a separate document (preferably a PDF), written on headed paper.

As an example, here is how you might format your press release and accompanying email for a book signing based on the list above.

Rachael Hardcastle

COMPANY LOGO
Author Name | Website | E-Mail | Telephone | Address

PRESS RELEASE
LOCAL AUTHOR TO SIGN LATEST RELEASE

ON [DATE/TIME] AT [STORE NAME] a popular local author is due to sign her latest release next month... [details about the event].

If you'd like to find out more about the author and any upcoming events near you, please visit [website link].

***

Good Morning/ Afternoon,

Please see an attached press release about [event/s]. These events will celebrate the release of the upcoming book, [name, genre, date of release and name of publishing house if relevant]. Additional dates and interviews may be added and will be listed at [website].

If you would like to arrange an interview or host an event, please feel welcome to contact me on the details below for further information.

Thank you for your consideration.

Kind Regards,
[Signature]

Marketing

Mission Statements

Your mission statement is an opportunity to outline who you are, what your goals are, your morals, values, ethics, culture, and what you have to offer.

Imagine you're introducing yourself at a public speaking event or someone at a book fair asks about your publishing company. What are you going to tell them? How are you going to squash all the important bits into a short, snappy introduction?

This is something quite personal, so there are no right or wrong answers. You as an individual can have a different mission statement to the company you run. To get you started, you can use the handy template below.

Consider where you would display this statement: social media, your website, your press kit, leaflets and posters.

My name is [name] and I'm a (genre) writer from (country). I believe that (beliefs) because/so (reasons/ explanation). My books are (what are they?), which you can find by visiting (website). I support (what?) because (reason), so I (action).

Press Kits

A press kit is sometimes referred to as a press pack or a media kit, and it's usually a digital set of promotional materials that are distributed (or made readily available online) to book stores, reviewers, the media and more. Press kits can also be physical, including print-outs, photographs, leaflets, etc., however, these are increasingly less popular because they are costly. It's important to put together at least a basic press kit so it's easy and convenient for people to find and use the information they may need about you, your book/s and your company. If they have to ask and wait a long time to receive these items, it doesn't inspire much confidence or professionalism!

- Mission statement and story. Who are you; what do you do and why do you do it? Include information about anyone else at your company/team with their permission; interviews with these people can make for an interesting read—quotes, too.
- Facts and figures. Include your book/author awards, certificates, qualifications.
- Photographs, logos and print-outs. You can include bookmark designs, poster and leaflet designs, infographics and head shots here.
- Product samples. You could include the first chapter of your new book, an FAQ list, bookmarks, merchandise and more.
- Press releases, interviews and news. If you have articles, links and other media involvement, you can include these. You should also include reviews and endorsements of note, plus testimonials.
- Social media and contact information.

Marketing Plans

A marketing plan contains a list of things you or your company will do to sell your product (aka your book). It needs to include a variety of sections such as:

- Budget
- Tactics
- Promotions you are running and discounts you are offering
- Sales predictions (how many are you going to sell and what is this prediction based on?)
- Publicity—in-person events and networking
- Media and press releases
- Platform/s including social media and your website
- Merchandise and promotional materials including your press kit, bookmarks and flyers
- Retailers and distributors you plan to use and why—what is your reach?
- Paid advertising vs free advertising
- Reviews/endorsements
- Joint ventures and collaborations
- Affiliates and sponsors
- Charities

It may be a good idea to write your marketing plan in sections; if you're unable to write one per book, then write one which includes as much information as possible about promoting your work in general. You may need to produce one for each genre you write in, because you'll market those in different ways and sell them to different audiences.

Start by including a picture of the book. You can use a 3D mock-up from a website such as bookbrush.com or diybookcovers.com and the book's blurb/description and price. Detail who your target audience is and why. How often will you measure how well your book is selling against your strategy, and how do you intend to do this?

Conclude the marketing plan by providing your author head shot and biography, then list your contact information.

Step Four - In Print

Bookmarks

The ideal size for a standard, low-cost bookmark is 85x200mm. Various companies can produce these for you.

If you opt for something that's double-sided, there are a few things you can do with the reverse, such as:

- Making the reverse a black and white image for children to colour in.
- Advertising one book on the front and another, similar title on the reverse.
- Use the reverse as your business card, which will save you money ordering anything additional.
- Leave the back blank so you can sign it at events and hand them out to readers for free. One-sided bookmarks are cheaper to produce.
- Have the same design on the front and back so the reader can see your latest release no matter which way they use it.
- Produce a series of bookmarks so your readers can collect them all, and feature illustrations of your characters.

- Print bookmarks on a thicker or laminated card stock, then use a hole punch and tassels (which can be ordered relatively cheaply online) and add a matching coloured tassel. You could even do this with charms or beads.

It's easier if you design your bookmark in advance, then export it as a PDF and upload it to a website when you're placing your order. You can use Canva or Kittl to design your bookmark free of charge. Their websites are canva.com and kittl.com.

When designing your bookmark, you should include a few details to ensure it's as attractive and informative as possible (for the side that advertises your latest release).

- Title
- Subtitle if applicable
- Series if applicable
- Author name
- Website and/or social media links
- Book cover
- Publisher name/logo
- Suitable images, colours and fonts for the genre

Consider the size of your bookmark based on the dimensions of your book, and whether you want something thicker and glossier or are happy with whatever the standard options are.

Leaflets

Leaflets are a great way to market to your readers after an event—it's something for that person to take home after meeting you, to ensure they don't forget who you are and what you write.

It's always better to give leaflets to people who look genuinely interested or who stop to say hello; some readers, particularly if they feel forced to take the leaflet, will simply dispose of it when they are out of sight. This not only wastes your marketing money, but it means you have potentially lost that reader altogether and it's a waste of paper. It's important to pick and choose who you approach when handing out marketing materials at an event.

You can use companies such as Vistaprint to produce batches of leaflets, which should have been created to look as professional as possible. Again, Canva is great for this. A5 is the perfect size. Anything larger, and you'd be moving into poster territory. Visit vistaprint.co.uk and check out the options.

- A3 is 297x420mm or 11.7x16.5" (large poster)
- A4 is 210x297 mm or 8.3x11.7" (poster)
- A5 is 148x210mm or 5.8x8.3" (leaflet/flyer)
- A6 is 105x148mm or 4.1x5.8" (small leaflet)
- A7 is 74x105mm or 2.9x4.1" (x-small leaflet)
- Postcards are 148x105mm or 5.8x4.2"
- Business cards are 85x55mm or 3.35x2.17"
- Bookmarks can be various shapes and sizes

Business Cards

Business cards are a must-have for all writers, whether you're published or not, and are approximately 3.35x2.17" in size. They should include your name, what you do (aka author/writer) and your contact information. Most business cards can be printed and delivered for a reasonable price. Companies such as Vistaprint or Banana Print (banana-print.co.uk) produce high quality cards at a reasonable cost.

Signed Photos

If you're also looking for an interesting giveaway option for school visits or events, another idea would be to order some prints of your author head shot as glossy photos. Apps like Free Prints allow you to order 50 free printed photos per month from your device, and you only need to pay the postage fee. Select one of your most professional and up to date photos and order a batch of them, then use a Sharpie to sign over the top. Visit Freeprintsapp.co.uk.

Sticker Rolls

Stickers don't have to include your logo. Why not order a roll of bookish-themed stickers for children, and hand them out at the same time as the leaflets? Parents get the info and children get a free sticker (which they will love!).

Marketing

Step Five - Common Sense

Business Hours

It may be useful when dealing with clients who live abroad to add your operating/business hours to your e-mails and your Facebook page. This prevents worry when someone doesn't receive an immediate response. After all, it might be three am for you; you can't answer the phone if you're sleeping. By informing your clients of your schedule, just like a shop has opening times, they know in advance that a lack of response is not due to ignorance. You may also want to add a line to a standard e-mail signature.

'Thank you for your e-mail. If this is in relation to a service, please allow up to 48 hours for a response during busy periods. I reply to all my e-mails personally and appreciate your patience.'

I pride myself in responding personally to all my e-mails. My clients never receive a standard template response to a quote, request or a letter—they get my undivided attention and assistance. Because I don't use an assistant, this can sometimes take a little longer, so I ask for patience, because it'll be worth it.

An auto-response let's the client know if they don't hear from me within 24 hours, I'm not ignoring them; I value their time and trust and will get back to them when I'm physically able to. If I go on holiday, my current clients are the first to know when I'll be returning so they don't feel abandoned, but I'll also update my e-mail signature and apply an auto-responder and inform new clients that I'm out of the office until further notice.

Consistency

Being consistent across your social media platforms is important. By consistent, I mean use the same profile photo, name/handle and bio wherever possible. If you have a long author name, you can shorten it or use something similar. People need to be able to find you everywhere quickly so they can like, follow and share at their leisure. Where you have fewer characters to play with, simply do your best.

- Facebook and Instagram - @rachaelhwrites
- Tiktok - @rachaelhwriter

If you post to one of your platforms, try posting to the others at the same time. You can link these together so it happens automatically, which can be done through your page's settings. We all prefer one platform over the other and because we only have two hands and one brain, we can't keep track of them all at once. Nor are you expected to, by the way.

Choose your favourite platforms and stick to updating those as often as you can. Two, maybe. Concentrate on those you prefer, and where most of your readers are. However, as the bio/about sections on all of them will include a website link, it's not hard for people to find you elsewhere.

You can use YouTube for videos of book signings, events and interviews, and from there you can embed them on a website and feature them in a newsletter.

Top Tip

If you don't ask, you don't get. *This* is my top marketing tip, and it looks at an author's confidence. We're quite often introverts, and sometimes feel our job is purely to write the book—leave marketing and promoting to the professionals, right? Wrong.

It only takes a minute to send an email, particularly if you already have handy templates and signatures set up. Scouting for interviews, bloggers and media opportunities doesn't need to be time-consuming. Don't wait to be approached; **be confident in your skills and talent** enough to approach people and ask for help (free of charge, if this is something they offer). As an independent, unknown author, you may be waiting a while for others to discover and approach you.

Ask local public figures and businesses to attend your event and/or endorse a book you think they would like. E-mail local bloggers, travel companies or events organisers, or contact them on social media. If they predict lots of people will attend the event, they may even agree to attend themselves because it's an opportunity. Just a few minutes of bravery and confidence could land you, as it did me, a television interview, radio interview/s and more.

Make a list of five people or companies that you can think of who may be interested in helping you out for free. Do your research, so when you approach them, it's clear you've made an effort. Take a few extra minutes to think of a few things that may prevent them saying 'yes', and write in a journal what your response would be if this happens. Can you cover those potential issues in the original enquiry?

For example, if the event is several miles away from where they are based, can you include a handy bus route/schedule or mention there is plenty of free parking?

Archery

What skills (besides writing) do you have to offer? If you are a creative, well-organised individual with fantastic computer skills, could you offer services to potentially help other struggling writers such as formatting or proofreading?

Evaluate your strengths and weaknesses. Use your strengths as an additional source of income to support your writing.

Identify and own your weaknesses. Nobody is perfect at everything. We all have them—work to improve in these areas before you put those skills to good use too.

A few examples may be:
- Web design
- Copy-editing
- Proofreading
- Formatting
- Cover design
- Public speaking
- Workshops/Talks
- School visits
- Reviews

What are you good at? List at least five skills—related to your business or field—that could provide you with an additional source of income while your book sells in the background.

Go ahead and make note of your strengths and weaknesses, too, so you can see where you might need a helping hand yourself. What are you going to do to increase your skills and deepen your knowledge?

Bestsellers

I'm sure the following questions will have crossed your mind once or twice, particularly if you use Amazon:

- Is my book still a bestseller if it reaches number one during a promotion?
- If a book reaches number one on Amazon during a free giveaway, is it still a 'real' bestseller?

The short answer: yes, it still counts! Some authors may argue against this—if you're not a New York Times bestselling author then it doesn't count, and of course most of those authors are published traditionally, which makes some indies feel becoming a bestselling author is an unreachable and unrealistic goal.

However, my arguments are all *for* the above. Because Amazon is such a huge, popular platform that if you reach number one in their eyes, it's a good indication that your sales are high and generally, there's lots of interest in your work.

Despite some niches on the Amazon platform being tiny, therefore having fewer authors in them competing for number one, reaching number one even in those is an achievement. Some of those categories might include 1,000 authors. Some of them may only include 150. Either way, if you can outsell even 100 other authors, I believe that's something to celebrate (given that most indie books usually only sell around 250 copies).

If it's your debut book, try not to worry about how many other authors you outsold. Just be pleased. This is why it's important to get your categories, genres, and keywords right when you publish the book, though. It's better to compete for first place in these smaller categories than in 'fiction' as a whole.

In my opinion, the bestselling status is about demand and popularity, regardless of the book's price. Sure, it might feel a bit more 'genuine' if you manage to reach number one having sold a hardback book at £15.99 to 150 people in a particular category, meaning

Marketing

150 people have willingly handed over money in exchange for something you created, but you can still have that feeling of accomplishment with a book on sale, or even free.

Have you ever tried to reach number one by pushing free downloads? It's harder than you think—on Facebook you might have around 100 friends (an example, not including your followers) and, despite your naïve hopes that every one of your friends and family members will click 'download' if it doesn't cost them anything, you'll be surprised how many will simply scroll past or look, then choose *not* to support you. It's nothing personal; their lack of participation could be for a variety of reasons.

- They saw your post/message at an inconvenient time and forgot by the time they got home.
- They don't have an e-reader or a device that supports similar apps.
- They genuinely aren't interested because you were never close—they're in your friend list, but it's so you can both be mutually nosey when it comes to what the other is up to these days. An old school friend or colleague, perhaps.
- They have 'liked' your page on Facebook but choose not to follow you, meaning they may not have even seen the post.
- They dislike being 'sold' to, even if the item you are pushing doesn't cost anything.
- Sending personal messages to people and asking them to do something can be seen as

invasive and unsolicited. I know it would annoy me if it happened more than once (twice at a push if it was something I genuinely had interest in).
- They share the device they read from, and your book would not be appropriate for the other person (such as a child).
- It's not a genre they like or will ever read, so they see no point in downloading it just to delete it later.
- Maybe it's a waste of time and will lead to you reaching number one without downloads from people who are invested in your work. Let's face it, sales from strangers always feel more special than sales from close friends.

Here are some other things to consider when you think about your views on the above argument:

- Do your readers even know the difference between an indie or traditionally published book? Lots of mine didn't until they met me in person and we had a chat about what I do and how I do it. They had no interest in the 'behind the scenes' part of publishing—as long as the book looked good and entertained them, they couldn't give a sh*t. A book is a book.
- Even if they *do* know the difference, do they care? Anyone not in the industry or familiar with the various publishing platforms may just be looking for something cheap and easy to read. If your book is free, discounted or even

full price and is visible to them at the right place and time, would they care that a large publishing house wasn't behind the production?
- Isn't a number one spot on any platform worth celebrating, no matter the logistics of how and why it happened? Rather than putting other indies down, simply offer a 'congrats' or say nothing at all.
- Don't be the grump that publicly questions someone's small achievement/s. I've been the victim of trolls before and while I see such comments at face value and try to ignore them, it does knock your confidence.
- Are you worrying about what other authors will think rather than readers? It goes without saying that if you're in writing groups on social media platforms like Facebook, you'll have exchanged conversations and perhaps page likes with other writers, meaning they will be seeing your posts and reading about your success.
- So, this links back to the previous three points in this section—rather than worrying how other authors will view your bestselling status (or reading any negative remarks they offer), think about how this will look to readers and other potential fans out there.

A bestselling status looks good, feels good and, in short, is good. Be happy and proud of it no matter the circumstances.

I know we can't all agree on the same terms when

it comes to what constitutes a 'real' bestselling status, but I'm a firm believer that if someone worked hard to achieve that status, no matter the circumstances, and *they* are proud, then we should support it.

Please, if you feel their bestselling status isn't 'real', don't publicly discuss this on their social media platform. Not only will it unnecessarily embarrass them and anger them, it's just not professional.

Trends

It may also be worth looking at the current trends to judge how well a book will sell at a current place/time.

For a while in fantasy and science-fiction, the popular themes were vampires and werewolves, love triangles, forbidden romances, witches and zombies—but maybe not all in the same book (though I can think of a few). By studying past and current trends, it's easier to predict what the next 'big thing' in fiction will be. However, my advice is *always* to write what you enjoy reading, and to write a book you would love to see on the shelf in your local store, rather than to write what's popular. Can you fill any gaps you feel are missing in fiction?

When I read a book, I can usually tell if the author didn't enjoy writing it.

Trends change and they do so quickly. Given that independent books can take twelve months to produce, by the time your release date rolls around, people could be reading something else. Purely writing to market may produce unreliable results.

Final Thoughts on Marketing

- Donate your books to your local library. Not only is your book then in circulation within your community, but readers will be pleased to see you're offering copies free of charge to good causes.
- Ask your friends, family and readers you meet to ask for your book in libraries so they order copies for their shelves.
- Run competitions and giveaways through your website. Give readers a chance to win signed copies of your book/s, merchandise and more.
- Create some awesome merchandise such as bookmarks, leaflets, business cards, stickers, pins, balloons, bookplates and clothing. You can also purchase branded USB sticks and other technology.
- Contact a local school and ask if you can deliver a creative writing workshop or a career day to their students free of charge. If they want to do the same the following year, introduce a small fee (because they will know from experience how good you are!).
- Be sure to have some giveaways ready for the children such as signed bookmarks, pens, or stickers.
- Share ten fun facts about you that readers may not already know. This allows them to build a personal connection to you.
- Be clear on what you want to achieve from

your writing. It's much easier to reach three clear, concise goals than ten half-arsed ones.
- Focus your efforts on your target audience rather than readers as a whole. Don't try to reach and please everyone because it's impossible. Once you know who you are selling to and why, you can tailor your techniques to best suit their needs.
- Don't spread yourself too thin, either. You'll wear yourself out.
- Write more books. The more books you have available, the better. If you're writing in a series, be sure to complete that series so invested readers aren't left disappointed.
- Do what works, then scrap what doesn't. Keep in mind, though, that it may not have worked due to timing or approach, so be sure to make notes and re-try at a later date.
- Leave your business cards, leaflets and bookmarks in various places (where you're not going to get in trouble for doing so). Ask at your favourite restaurants, coffee shops and stores if they have a notice board you can pin a leaflet or poster to, particularly if you have an event coming up.
- Write a press release and send it to local media and independent stores. Local literary festivals may also be interested in working with you.
- Independent Bookshop Week celebrates local stores every year. This may be something you'd like to get involved in. Their website is

Marketing

indiebookshopweek.org.uk.
- Can you discount your book so local indie stores can afford to stock copies and still make money?
- Gain reviews and endorsements from local public figures such as radio hosts and celebrities by writing to them and sending a free copy of your book in advance of its release date.
- Publish the book in as many formats as you can: paperback, hardback, e-book and audio. This way, you can reach more readers. If you're writing a non-fiction, can you also release a companion workbook? Would a companion colouring book also be of interest to readers?
- Model other success stories. What are popular/successful authors in your genre doing to promote their work? Why do you think their marketing styles work for them? Is there anything you can adopt and try yourself?
- Produce free worksheets and infographics for your website and allow people to download them easily as a PDF or share them with others.
- Read lots of marketing and business books to increase and improve your knowledge and skills.
- Read books in your genre as often as you can and examine what makes them so popular.

Merchandise Ideas

- Pens/Pencils
- Stickers
- Bookmarks
- Postcards
- Pins
- Tote bags
- Keyrings
- Charms
- Jewellery
- Notebooks
- USB
- Signed photos
- Balloons
- Bookplates (*sign these to stick them in books*)
- Colouring books/sheets
- Printables
- Bottle openers
- Mugs
- Coasters/Beer mats
- Clothing (t-shirts, hats, hoodies)
- Journals
- Workbooks
- Book page holder (wooden or plastic)

Make sure anything you do produce is of high quality and meets standards and any regulations in place.

Getting Paid Securely

If you're not only new to the world of publishing but also to technology in general, using your debit or credit card details online may be a cause for concern. You can Google 'how to tell if a website is secure' and find plenty of information, but generally take a look at the URL (the web address in the top search bar). If it begins with https rather than http, that site is secure.

Of course, I'm not an expert and there is always a risk when you enter your personal details online. Be sure when you do so that you are using your own computer so you know who has access and that it is fully password protected. Check to see who is around and avoid using free WIFI to log in to any accounts when you're in a public place.

Paypal is an alternative to having to input card details all the time, but not all platforms and websites accept Paypal payments. You can create a free Paypal account, then easily transfer money back and forth using an e-mail address. If you'd like to read more about Paypal, you can visit paypal.com. Of course, most platforms will also send you a payment via a BACS transfer (using your bank account number and sort code) or via a cheque, too.

Only *you* can make the decision with regards your payment methods, and only *you* can determine if a website is to your satisfaction beforehand.

From a marketing perspective, Paypal is common and well-known these days. Some readers—if buying direct through your website—will prefer to use this method for convenience and security rather than type in their card number.

If you're transferring a large sum of money for a service (or receiving one) it might also be wise to first transfer £1.00 to ensure it safely gets to where it needs to be before you transfer the rest.

I'd recommend receiving payment up-front before you supply goods and/or services, even if this is in instalments. Your customer (whether a reader or a client) will want to be sure they won't get ripped off. Just be a decent, honest professional. As an authorpreneur, you will want to be sure you'll get paid for all your hard work too, which is why instalments are usually a happy medium for all.

The End...

AND THAT'S IT... FOR NOW

Phew, Glad That's Over?

That's probably all you can take for now. Self-publishing seems easy on the surface but when you dig a little deeper, there's a lot to consider.

Try not to worry—there's absolutely no rush to publish your book. That's the great thing about being an indie; you can set your own deadlines, negotiate your own fees and perhaps even design your own covers and interior if you have the skills.

It should first and foremost be fun and enjoyable, particularly if the book you're writing isn't heading for the shelves but is, instead, for your own benefit.

The contents of this book are by no means the extent of self-publishing, nor my knowledge on the subject, but it's a good start and to be honest, it's *plenty* for you to consider if you're new to the publishing world. This sh*t is overwhelming.

By all means get stuck in to your research and ask around; speaking to other authors and people who have already made mistakes and had to fix them will help you to avoid them yourself. Get a variety of opinions and hear as many horror stories as you can handle.

Self-publishing has a bad reputation because of

books considered part of the 'slush pile', meaning unedited with poor covers and zero marketing. They let the side down and we need to prove that going indie doesn't mean publishing inferior work. For this reason, do your absolute best to produce a top-quality, professional product. It should stand proud beside a traditionally published book—readers shouldn't be able to tell the difference.

If this was indeed too much for you, don't be afraid to ask for help or to outsource work to a professional. **We all have our limits; there is no shame in knowing them.**

Of course, if you can be a 'hybrid' author and experience both sides (indie and traditional), that would be equally as awesome. Both routes have their merits and their let-downs, but until you experience each platform and publishing method, you won't be able to say for sure which is the best for you and your books.

- Which did you prefer?
- Which made you more money?
- Which gave you peace of mind?
- Which allowed creative freedom?
- Which met your expected level of involvement?

We are all different—our work has individual needs and you as a writer will find a natural path you're happy walking. This being the case, if after reading this book you decide self-publishing isn't for you, I won't be offended (and I'm confident you're therefore making the right decision). If you want brutal honesty, the self-publishing game isn't for everyone. In my opinion, some books should not have been released. It's never too late to fix mistakes—I learnt the hard way and there are probably still typos in this book despite all the work that went into it and all the people who were involved (thanks again, everyone!).

It's a shame when authors cut corners because these books have such potential. Now those stories may never see the success they deserve.

One Final Note...

As we part ways, I'll leave you with the following: **The universe may not give a sh*t about your book, but *you* do.** At this early stage, that's what's important, because with the right approach and preparation, we can encourage others to care in time, too.

You *can* do this. I know you can. You're not alone.

I've had my fair share of one star reviews, mean comments from people who have never written or even *read* a book in their life, and I've wanted to throw my failures and mistakes out the window only to give them a good kick around the garden. You're allowed the occasional tantrum—my gift to you.

Now get out there and publish your book—leave an inspiring mark on the world. Voice your truth, tell your story, and love what you do. From the bottom of my heart, I wish you every success.

RESOURCES

www.indiebookshopweek.org.uk - Independent Bookshop Week

www.banana-print.co.uk – Banana Print

www.stressfreeprint.co.uk – Stress Free Print

www.vistaprint.co.uk – Vistaprint

www.canva.com – Canva (graphic design)

www.authorcentral.amazon.co.uk - Amazon Author Central

www.readersfavorite.com - Readers' Favorite

www.diybookcovers.com - DIY Book Covers

www.bl.uk – British Library

www.gimp.org – GIMP

www.1001fonts.com - 1001 Fonts

www.goodreads.com – Goodreads (reviews and social)

www.gov.uk/copyright – Copyright Information (UK)

www.nielsentitleeditor.com/titleeditor – Title Editor (Nielsen)

www.nielsenbook.co.uk/isbn-agency – Nielsen ISBN purchasing

www.bisg.org/page/BISACEdition – BISAC codes

www.openoffice.org - Open Office

www.ads.google.com/intl/en_uk/home - Google Ad Words

www.paypal.com – Payments

www.grammarly.com – Editing software

www.autocrit.com – Editing software

www.literatureandlatte.com – Writing software

www.bulletjournal.com – Bullet Journaling

www.prowritingaid.com – Editing software

www.publisherrocket.com – Keyword software

www.kittl.com – Kittl (graphic design)

Resources

www.freeprintsap.co.uk – Free Prints App

www.ciep.uk/knowledge-hub/suggested-minimum-rates – Chartered Institute of Editing and Proofreading

www.writersandartists.co.uk - Writers and Artists Yearbook

www.ingramspark.com – Ingramspark

www.lulu.com – Lulu

www.kdp.amazon.com – Amazon KDP

www.pixabay.com – Pixabay (royalty free photos)

AUTHOR'S NOTE

I won't go on and on here, because those who deserve a thank you already know how awesome they are. Without some of you, I wouldn't be able to continue doing what I do; your support means the world to me, and I'm eternally grateful.

So, why the revised edition of '*The Universe Doesn't Give A Sh*t About Your Book*'? It can certainly still feel that way sometimes! But I wanted to add to this guide and update some of my tips, including my ABC of idea generation, a section about Story Beats, and a brief overview of how I got to where I am. As I wrote this new material, it occurred to me just how much effort and energy goes in to writing and publishing a book yourself, but it all starts with an interesting idea.

So as before, this thank you page goes out to the existing authors of the books lining my shelves, whose work has inspired and motivated and guided me over the years. And of course to all the aspiring authors out there; some of you I've met and chatted with during events, and some of you only know me through this reference book.

I believe in you all. You *can* do this.

Write on!

www.rachaelhardcastle.com

www.ingramcontent.com/pod-product-compliance
Lightning Source LLC
LaVergne TN
LVHW041614070426
835507LV00008B/238